The Authority of Scripture

A Report of the
Church of Ireland Bishops'
Advisory Commission on Doctrine

Published by
Church of Ireland Publishing
Church of Ireland House
Church Avenue
Rathmines, Dublin 6

Designed by Susan Hood
Cover design by Bill Bolger

© Representative Church Body and the contributors, 2006

All rights reserved. No part of this publication may be reproduced, stored in or introduced into a retrieval system, or transmitted in any form or by any means (electronic, mechanical, photocopying, recording or otherwise), without the prior written permission of both the copyright owner and the publisher

ISBN 1-904884-12-1

Printed by Paceprint Trading Ltd,
Dublin, Ireland

Introduction

IT SEEMS LIKELY that the precise function and authority of the Holy Scriptures within the life of the Christian Church has never been a matter for complete unanimity. What is more certain is that the Church of today - within many different traditions - is finding any such enquiry almost too difficult to confront, such is its potential for sharp and destructive divergence. In this, the Church of Ireland is no exception.

This report sets out, not so much to find a simple answer to the question as to recover a wholesome space for a mutual respect and courteous rapprochement between those differing approaches to biblical authority which are an inevitable element of our nature as Irish Anglicans. The theses concluding the report outline where this space for dialogue may be found. But these markers should be considered only in conjunction with the preceding series of essays provided by different members of the Commission.

Dr Andrew Pierce writes on the historical background to discussions on the authority of the Scriptures. This essay is followed by further critiques - from the differing perspectives of Revd Dr Maurice Elliott, Very Revd Dr Stephen White and Very Revd Dr Susan

Patterson, respectively - on how a doctrine of revelation, human experience and the life of the Christian community all contribute to a reasoned understanding of how the Scriptures are pivotal to the life of the individual Christian disciple and of the Christian Church. The final contribution is from Professor Nigel Biggar, who considers the use of the Scriptures in ethics. References and suggestions for further reading have been provided at the conclusion of each essay.

I wish to thank the other members of the Commission who gave so freely of their time, energy and expertise to this project. It should also be noted that, although each contribution is categorically the work of a particular author (and hence the precise perspective only of the individual contributor), much useful and lively conversation took place within the whole group on each of the themes covered. The agreement between all the members of the Commission on the concluding theses is open, sincere and, we believe, significant.

The report has been presented to the House of Bishops, which now commends it for study throughout the Church of Ireland.

✠ **Richard Meath and Kildare**
Chairman Bishops' Advisory Commission
on Doctrine

TABLE OF CONTENTS

      INTRODUCTION

7   MEMBERSHIP OF COMMISSION

9   CHAPTER ONE
      Where are we now? The contesting of biblical authority in historical perspective
      Andrew Pierce

53   CHAPTER TWO
      Scripture and experience: a creative tension
      Stephen White

67   CHAPTER THREE
      Scripture and revelation
      Maurice Elliott

103 CHAPTER FOUR
      Scripture and community
      Sue Patterson

141 CHAPTER FIVE
      The ethical 'use' of Scripture
      Nigel Biggar

165 SIX THESES ON SCRIPTURAL AUTHORITY

167 POSTLUDE

Membership of Commission

Chairman	Most Revd Dr Richard Clarke
Bishop of Meath and Kildare

Members	Revd Canon Dr Nigel Biggar
Professor of Theology and Ethics,
Trinity College Dublin.

Revd Dr Maurice Elliott
Rector of Shankill Parish, Lurgan,
Diocese of Dromore

Very Revd Dr Susan Patterson
Dean of Killala

Dr Andrew Pierce
Lecturer in Ecumenical Studies,
Irish School of Ecumenics, Trinity College, Dublin

Very Revd Dr Stephen White
Dean of Killaloe

1

Where are we now?
The contesting of biblical authority in historical perspective

Andrew Pierce

Taking our bearings

Travellers in unfamiliar territory must often find themselves wishing for one of the large-scale, viewer-friendly maps often found in tourist centres, complete with a bold arrow indicating that 'you are here'. Like a tourist-map, this chapter is intended to guide us into the issues raised by the continuing contesting of biblical authority, pointing out some key landmarks and accounting in broad terms for their significance.

Similes have their limits, however, and for reasons that will become apparent in due course, no attempt is made to provide a dogmatic arrow stating *exactly* where we are. A good deal of recent theology has been concerned with hermeneutics, which is the theory of interpretation. Texts do not 'contain' meaning in the same way that jugs contain milk; they require interpretation rather than simply being up-ended. This hermeneutical turn in theology is particularly important for the ways in which we appeal to biblical authority, as it has made us increasingly aware that 'we' - the interpreters of the text - interpret from within a context shaped by many prejudgements and value-commitments (some complementary, others conflicting), and that these inevitably shape our interpretation. Moreover, they always did. Every interpreter and every interpretative community operates both consciously and subconsciously from a particular perspective. Trying to interpret the biblical text obliges us to take seriously the ways in which our context shapes - and possibly skews - our interpretation.

So what shall this tourist map include? Not every tourist requires a deluge of detail, and therefore this map of the terrain provides the kind of information that is widely available from popular introductions to church history or biblical studies. There are, of course, many other important landmarks that could also be included in a more comprehensive - and significantly longer - guide. But, as theological tourists, even a small dose of historical information may help us to be mindful that ours is not the first generation to engage in heated debate on the kind of authority that we believe we are required to attribute to the Bible. And so this chapter briefly reviews some of the key themes that have emerged in Western Christianity's first two millennia of biblical interpretation: the emergence of the canon, debates over the relationship of Scripture and tradition, appeals to the fourfold sense of Scripture, the emergence of historical-critical methods, the modern anti-modernism of 'fundamentalism', and the so-called 'eclipse' (and recovery) of narrative.

The canon, canons and canonicity

When theology students first begin to study one of the biblical languages - say, for example, *koiné* Greek, the language of the New Testament - they encounter an extensive critical apparatus at the foot of each page of text. This carries information from an editorial committee, outlining how certain or how doubtful the committee finds variant readings of the text to be. Having thus barely begun to get to grips with a different language, the student is brought into contact with the complicated relationships between ancient biblical manuscripts that have to be pieced together, evaluated carefully and subjected to regular re-evaluation so as to produce an agreed text for a Greek New Testament. These manuscripts are in various forms - miniscules, uncials, papyri, lectionaries - and in a variety of collections worldwide, including the Chester Beatty Library in Dublin Castle.[1] Sometimes new manuscripts come to light, perhaps in libraries, or as a result of careful archaeological effort, or often entirely by accident, and then the Greek text must again undergo revision to ensure that as reliable as possible a text is provided for translation into other languages, such as English.

For those who are familiar with the Bible in their own language, catching even a glimpse of the textual complexity behind a well-known text can prove both exhilarating and unsettling. In view of the widely-acknowledged importance of agreeing a Greek text to readers of the New Testament in other languages, this world of textual scholarship is of enormous significance, even if its methods, results and uncertainties rarely, if ever, come to the attention of most readers of the Bible.

The discovery of new or variant texts also underlines the vulnerability of ancient scriptures: those discovered at Nag Hammadi in Egypt in 1945 had been buried to keep them safe, those found at the Dead Sea between 1947 and 1960 had been hidden in caves. That they were hidden suggests that they were perceived to be at risk. Many more, presumably, have been lost forever - whether deliberately or by accident - whilst others may possibly come to light in the future. As well as our loss of books and letters that were once authoritative in the early churches, we have also inherited a tradition of valuing a certain collection of books. Indeed, the plurality of authoritative texts circulating in the early Christian movement helps to account for one of its formative acts: the establishment of a canon, or list, of books that were to be regarded as authoritative scriptures.[2]

Like all the religions, Christianity constitutes a traditioning community in which sacred writings have played a key role in handing over the faith from one generation to the next: 'handing over' is the literal meaning of tradition. Later debates, particularly in the Western Church, have helped to forge a religious imagination in which 'Scripture' and 'tradition' stand opposed to one another. This unhelpful dichotomy effectively reduces these terms to a relationship of sheer opposition, and much of the scholarship of the past half century or so has sought to correct this by stressing the dynamic inter-connection between these two key theological themes. One residue from the long-standing either/or confrontation between Scripture and tradition is a tendency to overemphasize the unity of the completed canon as authoritative Scripture, thereby focusing scholarly attention away from the process by which certain books became 'scriptural,' and by which others did not receive this status.

The assumption that the Christian canon of Old and New Testaments appeared in the early church as a ready-made locus of theological authority came under sustained criticism at the end of the nineteenth century by authors such as H. E. Ryle, B. F. Westcott and A. von Harnack. In keeping with the idealist or evolutionary style of historiography that flourished at the time, these writers suggested that whatever unity the canon presented did not originate historically with the composition of the individual books themselves, but emerged over time - possibly over a *long* time - as books were recognized as authoritative because apostolic and therefore canonical.

Important consequences follow for our understanding of the early Christian movements. The historical Jesus, for instance, did not have an Old Testament, nor did he anticipate a New. As a Jew of the first century, however, he would have been familiar with many of the texts that Christians now call their Old Testament, and would have viewed these as authoritative. It is clear that many of his earliest interpreters - possibly echoing Jesus' own interpretation of his mission - also relied on certain of these texts in their proclamation of Jesus' identity and significance. That these writings existed at the time of Jesus and helped to shape his self-understanding does not necessarily mean that they constituted a formal 'canon' as we now understand the term. Current scholarly consensus is divided between those who consider that the traditional divisions of the Hebrew Bible into law, prophets and writings were closed to further additions on a progressive basis, with the writings remaining 'open' until about 100CE, that is, after Christianity had emerged as a religious rival to Judaism. Others, however, argue that both prophets and writings remained open as Christianity consolidated itself as a distinctive religious system. In either case, the idea that the closing of the canon of the Hebrew Bible was somehow linked with the post-Exilic reforms of Ezra (as was once widely held to be the case) is regarded as historically untenable, even though these reforms presuppose the closure of one of these divisions, namely the law.

The development of a New Testament canon took place slowly. The first list of all 27 books of our New Testament as authoritative writings comes from Athanasius of Alexandria's Festal Letter of 367. Indeed, this letter also provides evidence of the first use of the term 'canon' to denote a limit to the range of recognized authoritative writings. This may be the first extant 'canon', and its authority may have been confined to Athanasius' diocese, but we also know that collections of authoritative Christian writings - in addition to the Old Testament (including the Apocrypha) - were in circulation before then. Why?

In an influential account of early Christianity, Adolf von Harnack claimed that the emergence of the New Testament canon had been the 'orthodox' response to the Christian Gnostic, Marcion (viewed, somewhat improbably, by Harnack as a proto-Protestant theologian), who was an important teacher based in Rome between 140 and his death in c160. Marcion's views are known only from his opponents' writings (including such theological heavyweights as Irenaeus, Tertullian, Clement of Alexandria and Origen), but the trouble taken in refuting Marcion's position evidences his contemporary importance. Insofar as it can be recreated from its refutation, Marcion's system was dualistic, featuring conflict between the God of Love revealed in Christ, and the God of Law who had created this world. Marcion therefore rejected all forms of Christianity in which creation and redemption were identified as the purposes of the one God, and in support of this system, Marcion produced his own canon of ten Pauline letters plus a highly-edited version of Luke's gospel, purged of all its Jewish aspects. Von Harnack's thesis (which has been echoed by others) was that the Marcionite canon provoked orthodox Christianity into the activity of canonization.

The discovery of early Christian texts at Nag Hammadi makes von Harnack's thesis difficult to sustain, since the Nag Hammadi texts evidence a wide range of scriptural texts (i.e. texts regarded as authoritative by a Christian community) that clearly did not fall within the emerging 'orthodox' canon, such as the *Gospel of Truth* or the *Gospel of Thomas*. Long after Marcion's career had ended, it is clear that a wide range of scriptural texts was in circulation (perhaps thereby provoking the canon-defining letter of Athanasius?).

That a more restricted canon did emerge from a plurality of scriptures, and that certain texts were effectively lost to view for centuries, suggests that the process of canonization may have involved considerable conflict within the Church. Certainly, as more texts from this period have been uncovered, the more have concerns been raised about the political agendas of the victorious 'proto-orthodox' faction.[3] Ostensibly, the key reason why a book would be acceptable in the canon was due to its apostolic credentials. Some New Testament texts took a long time to gain acceptance as sacred Scripture: the book of Revelation provoked recurring unease, the Pauline authorship of the Letter to the Hebrews was questioned from an early date, and some texts - such as

Hermas' *Shepherd*, the *Wisdom of Solomon* and Tatian's *Diatessaron* - experienced fluctuating canonical recognition. Both the significance and limitations of these other texts are acknowledged in Athanasius' letter of 367 in his concession that Hermas' *Shepherd*, the *Didache* (which was rediscovered only in 1873), the *Wisdom of Solomon* and some Old Testament Apocrypha might be read for personal devotion.

Today's discussions evidence differences in approach to the issues of canon and canonicity to those made in the fourth century, as well as differences of emphasis as to whether it is form or content that takes priority in generating canonical meaning. For some, talk of canon is focused on the long, conflictual process of canonization, enforced - some will add - long ago for political reasons that may be evaded by attributing the outcome to the work of the Holy Spirit. For others, and for various reasons, exploring the origins of the canon is not a high theological priority: the canon is simply a given, defined by its finished form and content.

Many scholars currently view the closing of the canon with grave misgivings, and a number of important works has raised the question of what has been lost to the church by defining itself in this way. Within certain forms of Protestant Christianity, increasing awareness of the conflicts and debates surrounding the canonization process carries theological repercussions for the criterion of *sola scriptura*, since the canonization of these writings *as* Scripture was a traditioning act of the Church, with the first formal instruction to the Church to recognize a canon of 27 New Testament books being confirmed by Pope St Innocent I in 405.

Others, however, treat the existence of the canon as creative and as generative of meaning, rather than as inherently limiting. Perhaps the most famous recent example of this has been the 'canon criticism,' associated with Brevard S. Childs, James A. Sanders and others, in which the canon as a whole defines the primary literary context within which the biblical texts are to be understood. This emphasis on the role of canon as a 'semiotic mechanism' - to use George Aichele's phrase - is certainly helpful in addressing the question of the canon's meaning *now* as a literary system.[4] But whether one can successfully exclude the diachronic dimension of meaning (i.e. issues raised by the canon's emergence and subsequent interpretations, for instance: where did *this* canon come from? Is it adequate? And how would we know?), and still retain a satisfactory notion of canonicity - particularly since we have competing canons - is another question.

Scripture and tradition

Historically, oral tradition preceded the written tradition of Scripture: the earliest canonical gospel was written around 65-70 CE, and genuinely Pauline letters were written earlier in the 50s. Opposing Scripture and tradition in stark terms emerged during the polarized quest for theological authority during the Reformation in the Western Church. The criticisms of current church practice found in Martin Luther's (1483-1546) 95 *Theses* - his initial and hardly radical debating points - set him on a road towards the position he articulated during his debate with Johannes Eck, when he denied both papal primacy and the infallibility of General Councils in 1519. Within a short while Luther's reforms targeted the theological legitimacy of various church traditions in the name of the gospel message that he identified with the doctrine of Justification by grace through faith. These traditions included clerical celibacy, the offering of masses for the departed, the doctrine of Eucharistic transubstantiation and the challenging of papal interpretations of Scripture. Despite the robust rhetoric of the contemporary appeal to *Sola scriptura*, it is evident that Luther - and the other magisterial Reformers - operated with deep reverence for the apostolic tradition, and with a profound aversion to pretensions to apostolicity. Protestant theology thus developed a theological distinction between tradition that was apostolic (and therefore revelatory), and that which was post-apostolic, and which therefore needed to be judged by a revealed, apostolic, criterion. This distinction permitted the Reformers to accept the creeds of early Church tradition as representing truthful interpretations of Scripture.

The idea that the scriptural locus of revelation required to be supplemented by additional information, provided by extra-scriptural tradition, gained force from the teaching of the Council of Trent (1545-63) in its Fourth Session held in 1546. The Council distinguished between 'written books' and 'unwritten traditions', and, although it is probable that the Tridentine Fathers did not intend to teach that revelation was to be derived from two distinct sources, the so-called 'two-source' approaches to revelation (Scripture *and* tradition) grew to characterize Roman Catholic theology until the Second Vatican Council (1962-65), when an explicitly two-source schema was emphatically rejected. The extent to which arguments over Scripture and tradition revolve over mutually-exclusive caricatures in the Western Church during the period between Trent and Vatican II, is striking. One of the key texts of the twentieth-century Ecumenical

Movement, produced by the Faith and Order World Conference at Montreal in 1963, firmly dispenses with an unduly simplistic dualism in its careful distinction between three key terms 'Scripture, Tradition and Traditions':

> Our starting-point is that we are all living in a tradition which goes back to our Lord and has its roots in the Old Testament, and are all indebted to that tradition inasmuch as we have received the revealed truth, the Gospel, through its being transmitted from one generation to another. Thus we can say that we exist as Christians by the Tradition of the Gospel (the *paradosis* of the *kerygma*) testified in Scripture, transmitted in and by the Church through the power of the Holy Spirit.[5]

Symptomatic of this re-appraisal of the relationship between Scripture and tradition in the West has been a greater willingness among Protestant and Anglican writers to explore the importance of post-apostolic tradition, and a flourishing of biblical studies in Roman Catholicism. The positive significance of tradition is also underlined by hermeneutical theology, which reminds us that our current situation has been shaped by the tradition of reception that has been accorded to biblical interpretation in the past.

Senses of Scripture

The biblical texts contain a vast variety of materials. Some of this has been quarried exhaustively in early doctrinal debates, with minute passages seeming to carry considerable, and perhaps excessive, weight. For example, in the christological convulsions of the fourth century, God the Eternal Son was identified with Lady Wisdom whose role in the divine act of creation is recalled in Proverbs 8. Or the appeal to John 15:26 in order to formulate God the Holy Spirit's distinctive mode of being: since the Spirit is said to 'proceed' from the Father, a relationship of 'procession' appears in the discussion of inner-Trinitarian relationships. In addition to these texts on which the dogmatic spotlight has fallen, there are others which are either unremarkable or else downright awkward. Some of the more commonsensical statements in Proverbs are utterly banal: 'If you are cheerful, you feel good; if you are sad, you hurt all over', Proverbs 17:22; or there are contradictions in the text - for example, did the boy David kill Goliath, as in the well-known story in 1 Samuel 17? Or was the Philistine champion killed by one of David's men, Elhanan, as in 2 Samuel 21:19?[6] And there are many episodes which are ethically problematic. God's speeches of self-praise in Job 38-41, though magnificent, are largely beside the point; moreover God's gifts to Job of long life, ten children, great-great-grandchildren, plus twice his previous wealth, can hardly compensate for what the text acknowledges as 'the suffering the LORD had brought on him' (Job 42.11b). Or again, there is the disturbing conclusion to a well-known psalm (Psalm 137, 'By the rivers of Babylon...'), which is addressed to the city of Babylon: 'May the Lord bless everyone who beats your children against the rocks'. These examples can easily be multiplied, and their impact on readers (and their consciences) can scarcely be overstated.[7]

The first Christian theologian to address these difficulties explicitly was the Alexandrian scholar Origen (*c.*185-*c.*254), whose work *Peri archon/De principiis* echoed earlier Jewish allegorical interpretations by Philo (*c.*20 BCE-*c.*50 CE). For Origen, Scripture was a divinely inspired text, but just as humans are made up of body, soul and spirit, so too Scripture had literal, moral and allegorical levels of meaning. The last two categories were not always clearly distinguished by Origen, and often he operated with a simpler, two-fold distinction between the spiritual (moral or allegorical) and the literal levels of meaning, with the former carrying greater significance. This is not to suggest that Origen despised the literal meaning of the text. On the contrary, his scholarly activities included important efforts to establish reliable biblical texts so that the literal meaning could be apprehended. Origen noted that the scriptures were largely comprehensible and of moral value to most people, even to the uneducated. But, every so often, Origen observed, the biblical text *itself* provides some feature that interrupts a literal reading, for example a contradiction or a scandalous episode, and this interruption is an invitation to the more spiritually-minded to probe deeper to see what meaning the text is really disclosing. For Origen, all of Scripture, and not simply these 'interruptions', may be interpreted at a deeper, spiritual level of meaning, and the idea of a spiritual sense was to prove of great significance both in Origen's day and for long after. By claiming that the literal sense was not the only sense to be apprehended, Origen claimed attention from the platonic intelligentsia of the day for the biblical text: contradiction or scandal belonged only to the text's appearance, and not to the reality of the biblical message. There was, moreover, a Christological incentive for allegorical interpretation that arose in contemporary debates with Judaism: Origen argued that Jewish refusal to acknowledge Jesus' messiahship stemmed from an inability to interpret correctly the ways in which Jesus had fulfilled messianic prophecy. Allegory and typology were not, of course, new literary devices: the Letter to the Hebrews presents the temple priesthood as an anticipation of the priesthood of Christ; the non-canonical Letter of Barnabas, written in the early second century, relies on allegorical interpretation to present Christianity as the true successor and replacement for Judaism. Whilst allegorical interpretation may have offered the possibility of rescuing the God of the Old Testament from the criticisms of Marcion, it tended to push further to become a means of demeaning or possibly even terminating a theology of Jewish election: the true Israel was now the Church of Christ.

By the late Middle Ages, the idea that there were several distinct non-literal meanings to be gauged from a text had entered the mainstream of biblical preaching. Traditionally, these have been referred to as the 'senses' of Scripture, of which there are four. In addition to the literal sense, there is also the allegorical sense of a text which highlights a particular aspect of the literal sense, the anagogical sense to draw the readers' attention to the temporal future or to eternity, and the tropological or moral sense to provide guidance for living from the text.

Not all writers found appealing to four senses of Scripture helpful or even desirable. The hermeneutical strategy of the Antiochene theologians in the Patristic period preferred to focus on the literal and historical sense of the text (hence Antioch's stress on the humanity of Jesus Christ in the debates leading up to the Council of Chalcedon in 451). Even in the medieval period, many theologians insisted that close attention to the text was a necessary first-step in exposition, so as to guard against over-fanciful allegorization. The beginning of an end to appeals to the fourfold sense of Scripture came about during the Renaissance, when European humanism developed a fascination with the roots of its religious and intellectual life, and the exposition of classical texts assumed a new cultural significance. The achievements of Erasmus of Rotterdam (1466-1536) are symptomatic of these trends. Shunning allegorical approaches, Erasmus - together with Lorenzo Valla (1407-57) - borrowed methods of interpretation from the comparatively 'secular' disciplines of the classics, such as Greek and Latin philology. By concentrating on the literal and historical meanings of the biblical text, Erasmus underlined the importance of textual criticism by producing a corrected text of both the Greek New Testament and its Latin translation. This challenge to the accuracy of the hitherto normative Vulgate, in the interests of historical and textual accuracy, prepared the way for Luther's theological revolution in the early sixteenth century. Renaissance humanism's concern with textual analysis would issue ultimately in a characteristic genre of theological writing by Protestant Reformers and their successors, namely the biblical commentary.

The allegorizing impulse in biblical studies, with its concern to penetrate beyond the text's literal meaning, was undoubtedly an important resource for the Church and its scholars. Major theologians, such as Augustine, evidence the difficulties faced by the educated classes in reading the biblical text as something other than morally dubious tales, infelicitously expressed. A similar quest for a deeper, or more spiritual meaning than the literal suggests, still lingers in some devotional literature, although elaborately-constructed allegories (such as Bernard of Clairvaux's spiritual neutering of the 'Song of Songs') now seem a strangely convoluted way of reading to many readers.

The rise of the historical-critical methods

The term 'historical-critical methods' has a catch-all character to it, and is used to describe a handful of critical methods that have been applied to the biblical texts since - in very general terms - the nineteenth century.[8] This should not be taken to mean that in the previous centuries the historical origins of the biblical texts were ignored. The key criterion in the making of the canon, after all, was apostolicity and whether a particular writing was judged by the Church to be a product of apostolic witness (the writings of the so-called Apostolic Fathers proved, by this criterion, to be too late). Moreover, the allegorical tendency exhibited by the appeal to Scripture's fourfold sense, did at least start from the literal, though it often seemed to end up somewhere else altogether.

Modern historiography owes much to the Renaissance concern with establishing a critical edition of the original text, insofar as an original can be established, and with the priority it accorded to the literal and historical sense of that text. A characteristic assumption of the historical critical methods would therefore prove to be the normativity that it accorded to the original meaning of a text, together with a somewhat suspicious attitude towards the way the text has been interpreted subsequently. In view of this apparent preference for Scripture over tradition, it is somewhat ironic that one of the best-known ancestors of this approach was Richard Simon (1638-1712), a French Roman Catholic Oratorian priest, whose writings were presented as an attack on what has come to be known as Protestant scholasticism, in which biblical exegesis presupposed the logical consistency of the biblical text as an omnicompetent authority. Whilst Reformers like Luther and Calvin had operated with considerable critical freedom in their biblical interpretation, based on the interpretative key of the doctrine of justification, their successors had tended to apply the doctrine of inspiration indiscriminately. Rather than encountering the word of God in Scripture, the word of God had become simply identified with the biblical text. For Simon, this kind of biblicism ruled out, *a priori*, the very possibility of biblical criticism, whereas he claimed not to be dogmatically constrained and therefore free to pursue biblical criticism wherever his conclusions led him. On the basis of his research, Simon claimed that the Pentateuch had been compiled from a variety of earlier sources, and was not the work of a single writer, much less Moses.

Simon's approach anticipates much in the subsequent career of the historical-critical method. It was intended as critical history rather than as denominational propaganda, and it was undertaken with a strong apologetic intention to demonstrate the historical credibility of the biblical texts, properly understood. The term 'biblical criticism', though intended to suggest scholarly impartiality, still carries connotations of a negative impact on traditional, or allegedly traditional, belief and it is interesting that Simon's positive agenda was not fully-appreciated by the religious authorities of his day, a fate that has characterised a number of other important biblical scholars as the historical critical methods moved into the mainstream of exegesis.[9]

A suspicion that the real biblical history differed - perhaps radically - from its representation in the Bible, in subsequent tradition or in church dogma, is evident in many classically modern biblical interpreters. Isaac Newton, for example, famously found the New Testament to be inconsistent with the doctrine of the Trinity. By the nineteenth century, historical criticism was gaining new-found theological and philosophical significance, partly under the influence of Hegel's philosophy of history and the increasing importance placed on the discovery of Christianity's 'essence'. The quest for Christianity's essence attempted to account for the continuity of identity between normative, apostolic Christianity and the Church of the present day. On a post-Hegelian view of things, it would be historians - rather than theologians - who occupied the role of definers of Christianity's essence, and this essence was intended to provide the criterion for deciding what was, and what was not, authentic Christianity.

With definitions of Christian identity tied closely to the definition of a critical essence, as distinct from the traditional loci of authority in Scripture and church ministry, scholarly approaches to the biblical texts began to emphasize disunity in the scriptural corpus. Source criticism had been pioneered not only by

Richard Simon in France, but also in Germany by a variety of influential critics including G. Eichorn (1752-1827), W. M. L. de Wette (1780-1849) and J. Wellhausen (1844-1918), all of whom had worked on the texts of the Old Testament. The same concern with disunity was also apparent in New Testament study: F. C. Baur (1792-1860), for example, emphasised the conflict between Pauline and Petrine forms of early Christianity, and also argued - in order to keep 'Paul' consistent with himself - that only four of the Pauline letters in the New Testament were authentic (Galatians, 1 and 2 Corinthians, Romans).

In the study of the Gospels, source criticism identified a number of striking similarities between the first three Gospels (hence the term 'synoptic': these were Gospels that could be viewed together). The key question was how to account for the relationship between these texts: which evangelist had access to which other gospel or gospels? The widely-accepted answer to the synoptic problem is that the first Gospel to be written was that of Mark, probably sometime between 65 and 70. The text of Mark's Gospel was available to Luke and Matthew when they were writing, probably within ten or twenty years' time. In addition to Mark (and to material unique to either Matthew or Luke), these evangelists shared another common source, made up mostly of sayings of Jesus plus material concerning the Temptation and John the Baptist, which is usually referred to as 'Q' from the German word *Quelle*, meaning source.

Having broken down the once-unified text into its constituent sources, a further critical step came from Form Criticism, pioneered particularly by H. Gunkel (1862-1932) in Old Testament study, and by his pupil R. Bultmann (1884-1976) in New Testament study. A key insight of form criticism is that a literary form presupposes a social context, in German *Sitz im Leben* (literally, situation in life), and that, using the text as a window, it is possible to peer through the text and recreate its original social setting. A psalm, for example, presupposes a liturgical community bringing its social and theological concerns together in an act of worship in a type of literature - or genre - that makes it possible to generate certain sorts of meaning. For form critics, it is the literary form, with its socially-agreed conventions, rather than individual 'authors,' that is responsible for the generation of meaning. This insight carried far-reaching consequences, particularly in the application of form criticism to the gospels, as critics argued that words placed on the lips of Jesus by the evangelists, were to be seen as products of the early Christian movements, reflecting their own situations and not that faced by Jesus of Nazareth.

If both source and form criticism worked by emphasizing the disunity of the biblical text, Redaction Criticism - a term coined by W. Marxsen - focused attention on the unifying work of the editors who brought together various sources in order to compose a particular text. For example, both Matthew and Luke edit part of the potentially problematic storyline that they had inherited from Mark, since Mark presents Jesus receiving John's baptism 'for the forgiveness of sins' (Mark 1:4-11; compare Matthew 3:4-17, Luke 3:1-22. In John 1:19-34, Jesus avoids baptism at the hands of John altogether). Like Matthew and Luke, those who edited a text did so from a particular standpoint, and by concentrating on that standpoint, redaction critics were able to delineate the theological agendas at work in the editorial process. Paradoxically, therefore, just as uneven features in a text had highlighted the presence of sources, redaction critics attempted to demonstrate the extent to which editors had succeeded in fitting together the original sources.

These three historical-critical methods of biblical interpretation have in common the assumption that there is an original meaning of the biblical text which can be extracted and which is, in some sense, normative. The source critic looks to the various sources contained in the finished work as the text closest - chronologically speaking - to the original and now unreachable oral tradition. Recreating the author's - or better, compiler's - intention, therefore, is the source critic's priority when expositing the meaning of a text. For the form critic, however, a text is not the product of an author or compiler, but of a community that operates with certain conventions governing the meanings of different literary forms, or genres. Recreating the original communal setting - the *Sitz im Leben* - of a text is the defining feature of an adequate interpretation. Finally, the redaction critic looks to clues within the text in order to clarify the theological assumptions at work when the component parts of the text (wherever they had come from originally) were ordered into a relatively coherent whole. The first two methods highlight differences within the text, the third presupposes them.

Despite their concern with recreating an accurate history of the world behind the text, part of the impact of the historical-critical methods was to produce a disorientating and widening gap between the historical figures and events represented in the biblical texts and the creation of the texts in which readers now encountered them. Thus, for example, the parable of the Good Samaritan emerges from the hands of the critics as a Lukan composition, and not a story told by the historical Jesus, though obviously inspired by the Christ event. This apparently negative impact of criticism on what was assumed to be traditional interpretation inevitably caused difficulties when it reached a public hitherto unaware that history and dogma seemed to be living increasingly separate lives. These difficulties may account in part for a frequently acknowledged gap between the widely accepted scholarly consensus on the historical origins of the biblical texts, and the popularly-presented accounts of biblical history in, say, preaching. There is, however, a world of difference between finding the results of historical-critical scholarship uncomfortable, and simply refusing to accept its findings or its methods. This latter stance has come to characterize a growing religious trend in our day, usually referred to as fundamentalism, to which we now turn.

Modern religious anti-modernism

Fundamentalism is a deeply problematic word. Whilst some people, including some Christians, are proud to describe themselves as fundamentalists, others see the term as intrinsically dismissive of those so-named. Scholarly treatment of this religious phenomenon struggles (although not always successfully) to avoid treating fundamentalism as a cognitive defect to be remedied. The term possesses an elasticity that makes it possible to apply it far beyond its point of origins. Bizarrely, although the term 'fundamentalism' has its origins in North American Protestantism, as a result of two events, the 1979 revolution in Iran and the September 11 attacks in the USA, it has been increasingly associated with Islam, both in popular culture and in religious scholarship. To believe, however, that the psycho-social phenomenon of 'fundamentalism' is limited to any one religious tradition is a mistake. All religious traditions are presently experiencing analogous phenomena, described - however inadequately - by the term fundamentalism. This places an onus on biblical interpreters to see why our present and recent past have been especially conducive to the exponential growth of this kind of religiosity, along with its characteristic modes of appealing to Scripture.

The original fundamentalist movement arose in the United States of America during the late nineteenth and early twentieth centuries, taking its name, in July 1920, from *The fundamentals*, a series of essays published between 1910 and 1920.[10] A defining feature of this movement was its rejection of the findings of the historical-critical methods in biblical studies, which seemed to call in question the historicity (and 'therefore' the truth) of certain biblical references. The 'five points of fundamentalism' (an inversion, in many respects, of theological liberalism's 'essence' of Christianity) emerged in the late nineteenth century, affirming particular beliefs that critical theology either denied, or else failed to prioritize. These beliefs included plenary verbal inerrancy of Scripture, the divinity of Jesus Christ, Christ's virginal conception, a substitutionary theology of atonement, and Christ's physical return in glory. The reactionary nature of these 'points' is readily apparent, and it is striking that *The fundamentals* first went to press in the same year as the World Missionary Conference met at Edinburgh, thereby setting in motion the institutional face of the ecumenical movement which is in many respects fundamentalism's 'other'.[11]

By affirming plenary verbal inspiration, and by equating this with inerrancy, Christian fundamentalism attributes a revelatory significance to the biblical text that is similar to the Islamic understanding of the *Qu'ran*, in which the words in the text are the very words of Allah to Mohammed. Christian approaches to the Bible as the word of God have traditionally been more circumspect, distinguishing between the primary reference of the phrase 'word of God' (i.e.

Christ the Word incarnate) and the textual witness to that Word. Christian fundamentalist appeals to inspiration - as a guarantee of inerrancy - also diverge from the pluriform models of inspiration exhibited throughout Christian history which sought to safeguard the possibility of inspired texts being put to less-than-inspired ends.

Fundamentalism, however, is more than a method of biblical interpretation. It is also a symptom of other trends and this has made it possible to export the term fundamentalist meaningfully to a wide range of other contexts. It may also explain why political scientists and sociologists, rather than theologians, are to the fore in scholarly approaches to fundamentalism. In his important study, Bruce Lawrence characterises fundamentalists as being modern yet anti-modernist, a distinction that he draws from Marshall Berman. According to Berman, modernity is simply our socio-cultural setting, in which we undergo constantly changing experience and in which old securities inevitably evaporate with the passage of time, hence his book's title *All that is solid melts into air*, a phrase made famous by Karl Marx. A modernist, by contrast, is a modern who has internalised the relativizing ideology of modernity, and who feels fully at home in the modern world. Anti-modern*ists* reject modern*ism* from a standpoint within modernity, and therefore Lawrence argues that whilst fundamentalists are modern, they are not modernists. Disquiet over the modern project - sometimes referred to as its post-modern critique - has thus generated a psycho-social context in which the religious aspects of modern anti-modernism are more likely to flourish.[12] This point is made clearly by Richard T. Antoun:

> ... fundamentalism is a reaction, both ideological and affective, to the changes in basic social relationships that have occurred on a worldwide basis as a result of the social organizational, technological, and economic changes introduced by the modern world and as a result of the historical shift in power relations that has occurred over the last two hundred years in that world.[13]

Hence, fundamentalism in a variety of different religions professes a 'traditional' form of belief that turns out on closer inspection to be an anti-modernist positivism, rather than traditional in a recognizable, historical sense. This capacity to appeal both to head and heart whilst offering a secure refuge from the ideology of modernism, is underscored by Thomas Meyer's term 'identity mania', which he defines as a problematic development in the otherwise healthy pursuit of a secure sense of identity.[14]

The challenge from fundamentalism for biblical

interpretation may therefore prove most significant in what it discloses about our age, rather than the particular exercises in exegesis that it undertakes in support of its various global projects ranging from promoting creationism to combating liberalism and ecumenism. In an age of identity mania, the challenge for the Churches is to interpret its sacred texts responsibly so as to address - rather than merely echo - the spirit of the age.

The loss and recovery of narrative

Both fundamentalism and the historical-critical methods have their roots in the pre-suppositions of much nineteenth-century positivistic historiography, with its naïve attachment to 'facts' which could be described by means of the tool that is language. At the start of the twentieth century, however, a philosophical development - the turn to language - was about to begin, and this would have far-reaching theological consequences.

Symbolic of the linguistic turn is the work of a Swiss linguist, Ferdinand de Saussure, who in 1915 published his *Course in general linguistics*. Saussure re-orientated linguistics away from a predominantly historical study of the evolution of linguistic forms through time (a diachronic approach) to a concentration on the way in which language now functions as a system (a synchronic approach). He distinguished between *langue* and *parole*, usually rendered 'language' and 'discourse' in English: *langue* refers to language as a coherent system and to the rules that maintain coherence within the system; *parole* is the way in which that system appears to us in specific instances of words and sentences. Linguistic meaning, according to Saussure, was not satisfactorily dealt with by historical exploration of what a word meant or intended in the past: meaning should refer to the function of particular linguistic signs in a given system. Significantly, therefore, Saussure discussed linguistic meaning without reference to an 'original' meaning (whether supplied by an author or a community), and without reference to extra-linguistic reality. Linguistic signs therefore are defined with reference to other signs, which are defined with reference to other signs and so on, *ad infinitum*.

Saussure's approach - known as structuralism - carried wide ramifications for biblical studies, even for those who did not sign-up as full-blooded structuralists. It offered an alternative approach to texts for those biblical scholars who were dissatisfied with either the historical positivism of the historical-critical methods or the existentialist refinement of those methods championed by Rudolph Bultmann (see p. 33 above). Perhaps more importantly than its specific features, structuralism symbolizes an important change of attitude towards language and its relationship to human experience. Much nineteenth-century philosophy operated with the assumption that language was primarily a tool through which human experience could be expressed: experience preceded linguistic expression. The turn to language inverted this relationship by stressing the significance of language as *langue*: human beings do not simply use language, they are shaped by language and in some sense their experience is prescribed by language. Hence a great deal of twentieth-century philosophy has turned to examine forms of language - tropes, metaphors and symbols, for example - with a sharpened awareness that these are not simply decorative features in a text (as Aristotle had once claimed) but are irreducible configurations of experience that demand interpretation.

Strong echoes of structuralism's preferential option for synchrony over diachronic approaches are evident in the Yale theologian Hans Frei's approach. In 1974, Frei published an important work that was symbolic of new directions in theological engagement with Scripture, *The eclipse of biblical narrative*. He argued that, in the period since the seventeenth and eighteenth centuries, biblical interpretation had taken a spectacularly wrong direction by losing sight of the narrative medium of Scripture. Modernity's concern with first establishing an historically accurate text and then assessing the biblical stories on the basis of their historical veracity (or otherwise), indicated to Frei that the Bible had been read by moderns primarily as an historical resource for reconstructing the world in which the text originated. The text had become a means to an historical end, rather than an end in itself.

Pre-modern readings of Scripture, according to Frei, had worked, not by breaking down the narrative flow into its constituent original sources or its literary forms, but with larger narratives which had shaped the worlds of Christian imagination through history. This was a theological - rather than historical-critical - way of reading Scripture, in which key elements of theological vocabulary were to be understood according to their situation in the stories of God's engagements with the world, set within the larger biblical story that runs from the chaos preceding Creation to the heavenly Jerusalem. Rather than a concern with the meaning of the biblical stories themselves, however, moderns have treated these stories as narrative illustrations of something *else*, some 'religious' or moral truths, which must be extracted from their narrative setting in order to be apprehended.

Frei's approach has been influential amongst a variety of theologians, often dubbed post-liberals, such as Ronald Thiemann, William Placher, Stanley Hauerwas and George Lindbeck, all of whom are concerned to restore story or narrative to a place of centrality in Christian theology. Part of the attraction of the post-liberal agenda is its concern to bridge the gulf that opened up in the modern period between biblical studies (concerned with historical and literary criticism) on the one hand and with systematic theology (concerned with philosophy) on the other. Moreover, post-liberalism is eager to stress its post-critical credentials. Unlike fundamentalisms, which may reject both the methods and results of historical-critical biblical interpretation, a post-liberal theology, such as Frei's, presupposes the findings of critical biblical interpretation in its quest to ask what a particular text means.

The recovery of narrative in biblical interpretation is evident in a number of developments in much late twentieth-century theology. The rise of a specifically narrative criticism has fostered a dialogue between secular literary critics and biblical scholars on the ways in which texts generate meaning.[15] Moreover, a turn to narrative in continental European philosophy has emphasized that not only does narrative produce meaning in literary texts, it also shapes both those selves and communities that engage with particular narratives, and provokes them to develop particular identities in response to those literary narratives.[16]

Conclusion

It is clear, from even the most basic of historical surveys, that reflection on the authority appropriate to the Bible has provoked recurrent conflict within the Church, and that this conflict presents itself to us in the biblical text itself. In a helpful phrase, the distinguished Dutch theologian Edward Schillebeeckx refers to the Church as 'an interpretative community'.[17] If the Churches of the twenty-first century are to take seriously the implications of this phrase, then they would do well to reflect on the unavoidability of conflict within Christian interpretative communities. As certain debates develop into conflicts (whether ethical, liturgical or political etc.), it may prove that the challenge for the Churches is not simply to work out which 'side' in a given debate is more faithful to biblical authority. It is hard to imagine a scenario in which either side in an ecclesial conflict would not claim to respect the authority of the Bible.

Perhaps a greater challenge for the Churches is to take seriously their role as interpretative communities, in which not only agreement but also disagreement on matters of significance is as inevitable as it was in Paul's Corinthian Church. Learning to manage our conflicts of interpretation within the Churches extends theology far beyond its traditional concerns with doctrinal theology and biblical studies, and raises questions of power and of the ways in which fallible human beings exercise power in their no-less fallible institutions.[18]

Standing on the threshold of the twenty-first century of the common era, the Christian Churches have inherited sacred texts that infuriate, baffle and inspire many within and outside the Churches. A first task in interpreting these ancient writings is the modest acknowledgement that we are not the first to find ourselves struggling with these texts. Trying to establish the ways in which the Bible is authoritative - as opposed to simply affirming *that* it is authoritative - has proven costly and difficult to the Churches in the past: as well as provoking scholarly debate, it has contributed to violent dissension and to the scandal of ecclesial disunity.

It is evident that the Churches do not - and did not -

read the Bible in a cultural vacuum. Understandings of biblical authority, and understandings of how the biblical texts are to be interpreted, need constantly to be set in a critical dialogue with our understanding of how the various ideologies of our world shape us as interpreters. The great Reformed theologian Karl Barth told his students that they should do theology with a Bible in one hand, and a newspaper in the other. Sustaining that tension, between understanding the sacred text and understanding the world in which that text is read, has often proven uncomfortable for the Church in its first two millennia. If we are willing to learn from our past, then our affirmations of biblical authority may reasonably anticipate future discomfort for the Churches. Perhaps the anticipation of future friction will also provoke Christian interpretative communities to develop - together - ways to 'stage' conflict in which the participants are not allowed to forget that their conflict, since it is concerned with truth, is also an expression of communion.

References:

1. See David Hutchinson-Edgar, *Treasuring the word: an introduction to biblical manuscripts in the Chester Beatty Library* (Dublin: Townhouse, 2003).
2. Forming a canon did not, however, solve the problems of plurality within Christianity, since not all Christians - then or since - agree on a common canon. For a detailed treatment of the formation of the New Testament canon - and the various intermeshing factors (philosophical, liturgical, doctrinal, etc) involved - see Bruce M. Metzger, *The canon of the New Testament: its origin, development and significance* (Oxford: Oxford University Press, 1987).
3. The term 'proto-orthodox' is proposed by Bart D. Ehrman, *Lost Christianities: the battles for Scripture and the faiths we never knew* (Oxford: Oxford University Press, 2003).
4. George Aichele, *The control of biblical meaning: canon as semiotic mechanism* (Harrisburg, Pennsylvania: Trinity Press International, 2001).
5. The text: 'Scripture, tradition and traditions', written in 1963, is translated in Günther Gassmann (ed.), *Documentary history of faith and order: 1963-93*. Faith and Order Paper No. 159 (Geneva: WCC Publications, 1993), p. 11.
6. The re-telling of this story by the Chronicler permitted some editorial tidying: 1 Chronicles 20:5 claims that it was Lahmi - Goliath's generously-built brother - who met his end at the hands of Elhanan.
7. One of the classic examples is Søren Kierkegaard's revulsion *and* fascination at Abraham's 'binding' of Isaac (Genesis 22) in his 1843 essay, *Fear and trembling*.
8. There is a useful account of earlier anticipations of the historical-critical methods by Klaus Scholder, *The birth of modern critical theology: origins and problems of biblical criticism in the seventeenth century* (London: SCM: 1990).
9. For example, W. Robertson Smith in Scotland in 1881, C. A. Briggs in the USA in 1893, the *Lux Mundi* essayists in the Church of England in 1889, and the Modernist crisis in Roman Catholicism in the early years of the twentieth century.

10. R.A. Torrey (ed.), *The fundamentals* (2 vols. Grand Rapids: Baker Books, 2003).
11. There is a useful conspectus of fundamentalism as a global phenomenon in Martin E. Marty and R. Scott Appleby, *The glory and the power: the fundamentalist challenge to the modern world* (Boston: Beacon Press, 1992).
12. Bruce B. Lawrence, *Defenders of God: the fundamentalist revolt against the modern age* (San Francisco: Harper and Row, 1989); Marshall Berman, *All that is solid melts into air: the experience of modernity* (New York: Simon and Schuster, 1982).
13. Richard T. Antoun, *Understanding fundamentalism: Christian, Islamic and Jewish movements* (Walnut Creek, Lanham, New York and Oxford: Altamira Press, 2001) p. 11.
14. Thomas Meyer, *Identity mania: fundamentalism and the politicization of cultural differences*. Critical Studies in International Development II (New Delhi: Mosaic Books, 2001).
15. See Mark Allen Powell, *What is narrative criticism? A new approach to the Bible* (London: SPCK, 1993).
16. A point emphasized by Paul Ricoeur, whose philosophy exhibits sustained engagement with the literature of biblical and theological studies. See his *Oneself as another*, as translated by Kathleen Blamet (Chicago and London: University of Chicago Press, 1992), especially pp 113-168.
17. Edward Schillebeeckx, *Church: the human story of God* (London: SCM, 1990).
18. The idea that churches should 'stage', rather than avoid conflict, when truth is at stake, was central to the ecumenical vision of the curiously-neglected theologian Ernst Lange. See his: *And yet it moves: dream and reality of the ecumenical movement,* as translated by Edwin Robertson (Grand Rapids, Michigan: Eerdmans, 1979).

For further reading:

A treasure in earthen vessels: an instrument for an ecumenical reflection on hermeneutics (Geneva: World Council of Churches, 1998)
David Brown, *Tradition and imagination: revelation and change* (Oxford: Oxford University Press, 1999)
idem., *Discipleship and imagination: Christian tradition and truth*

(Oxford: Oxford University Press, 2000)

Hans Frei, *The eclipse of biblical narrative: a study in eighteenth and nineteenth-century hermeneutics* (New Haven and London: Yale University Press, 1974)

Garret Green (ed.), *Scriptural authority and narrative interpretation* (Eugene, Oregon: Wipf and Stock, 2000)

idem., *Theology, hermeneutics, and imagination: the crisis of interpretation at the end of modernity* (Cambridge: Cambridge University Press, 2000)

Gerard Loughlin, *Telling God's story: Bible, Church and narrative theology* (Cambridge: Cambridge University Press, 1996)

Gabriel Josipovici, *The book of God: a response to the Bible* (New Haven and London: Yale University Press, 1988)

Stephen Prickett, *Narrative, religion and science: fundamentalism versus irony, 1700-1999* (Cambridge: Cambridge University Press, 2002)

Sandra M. Schneiders, *The revelatory text: interpreting the New Testament as sacred Scripture* (San Francisco: Harper, 1991)

Gerd Theissen, *Traces of light: sermons and Bible studies* (London: SCM, 1996)

John Webster, *Holy Scripture: a dogmatic sketch* (Cambridge: Cambridge University Press, 2003)

Frances Young, *The art of performance: towards a theology of Holy Scripture* (London: Darton, Longman and Todd, 1990)

2

SCRIPTURE AND EXPERIENCE:

A CREATIVE TENSION

Stephen White

THE 'AUTHORITY OF SCRIPTURE' is a familiar phrase, but it is capable of a wide variety of interpretation, not least because although we all know clearly enough what Scripture is, the concept of 'authority' is more elusive and susceptible of almost endless permutations of meaning. It seems prudent, then, to attempt to define, or at least clarify somewhat, what is meant by authority in the present discussion.

Scripture is said to have authority or to be authoritative then, in the sense that it is something which can generally be relied upon and which is accurate and faithful in certain foundational ways. By this is meant that it reflects the story of humanity's encounter with God and God's with humanity, in ways which reveal to us insights and truths about the nature of God and about the appropriate human response(s) to that revealed nature. It does not mean that Scripture is verbally inerrant or 'divinely dictated'; and it equally does not mean that we are forbidden to interrogate Scripture or even at times to argue with it on the basis of other human experience of God or the demands of reason. The authority of Scripture requires us to reckon seriously with it, but while it may make us a people of the book it does not make us prisoners of that book.

Turning to the question of the authority of Scripture, then, the central problem with any attempt to discuss the subject is the crucial question: whence does its authority come? Does Scripture have an inviolable authority as coming from God, or does it only have authority insofar as we are willing to grant authority to it? Does it have an authority of its own, regardless of our experience and response to it, or is it itself in some way subject to that experience and response? Or is there, perhaps, some other way of expressing its authority without resorting to quite such a stark either/or scenario? It is somewhat like the question posed by Jesus as to the provenance of John's baptism:

> They discussed it among themselves and said, "If we say, 'From heaven', he will ask, 'Then why didn't you believe him?' But if we say, 'From men' - we are afraid of the people, for they all hold that John was a prophet". So they answered Jesus, "We don't know".[1]

The difference here, however, is that for the sake of the Church and of every individual within it, we need to find a way of saying something rather more positive than simply with the chief priests, the teachers of the law and the elders, 'We don't know'.

An initial objective might be to illuminate some middle-ground for discussion by attempting to avoid either one of two mutually exclusive extremes. The first is the view that the Bible is a collection of interesting texts from ancient history (some more interesting than others and some positively dangerous), from which the individual may pick and choose for him or herself those portions that are deemed (by that person themselves) to be most conducive to a happier, calmer or more fulfilled life. And by the same token the individual also has the right to choose which portions should be ignored or rejected. Thus everyone is free to decide on their own personal, individualised and customised canon of Scripture.

The second extreme view, which we have already effectively disowned in the first paragraph of this discussion, is that the Bible was, in effect, dictated by God, in such a way that the intermediary human agencies were incapable of misinterpreting or mishearing the divine message. The Bible is, literally, God's own word, and verbal inerrancy is assured.

It would help the cause of finding a middle-ground

greatly if these two extremes could be quickly ruled out, one as useless and the other as profane. The first is useless because it simply encourages all and sundry to reinforce their individual spiritual and moral predispositions, and then to define as Christian (in their terms) anything which happens to appeal to them. The second is profane because it accords to a multitude of individuals and generations of a particular community the grace of an absolute infallibility and inerrancy in their 'writing up' of the Bible.

If there is any measure of agreement as to the existence of this middle-ground, such that even those who may have some sympathy with a more outspoken (though plainly not totally extreme) view, might be able to give it their support, then there is arguably, a viable way into the puzzle of authority which leads us to what this essay will attempt to demonstrate, a realistic and satisfactory approach to and engagement with Scripture. This is to look critically and in rather more detail at the shortcomings of both of the alternatives outlined above - which are, in essence, the two most common opposing views of scriptural authority - and then to ask in the light of these shortcomings what other approach there may be which avoids the excesses of both sides.

First, then, it is, I think, axiomatic to the post-modern (and indeed before that to the modern) mind, that Scripture cannot simply have an innate, overriding God-given authority which may not be questioned or challenged. It should be stressed here that this is not at all the same thing as denying all authority to the Bible or denying that there is divine inspiration in Scripture. It is not the presence of inspiration and authority which is at issue, but the nature of that inspiration and authority. The holding of a doctrine of verbal inerrancy, for example, requires the belief that God 'dictated' the Bible to human scribes who were therefore incapable of error. Such a view demands a degree of biblical fundamentalism which is no longer a realistic option for us. It requires us to be so completely fundamentalist that we acknowledge the equal authority of **all** parts of Scripture (since according to this view they are all divinely inspired) and this is a position to which not even those who would call themselves fundamentalists actually adhere to in practice. Further than this, though, and regardless of how individual Christians may view the Bible, it is patently obvious that, pragmatically speaking, Scripture exercises no authority whatsoever over the lives of vast numbers of people. Thus even if we wish to claim that Scripture has some sort of intrinsic authority this obviously needs to be complemented by our response to it which acknowledges that authority and is therefore able presumably to exercise judgement as to in what precisely that authority consists. At the very least then we can say that Scripture is not an authority 'over against' us to which we are simply subject willy-nilly, but an authority with which we are profoundly in dialogue as to the exact nature and scope of that authority.

If fundamentalism is one untenable extreme, then the other extreme of what we might call 'ultra-criticalism' is equally untenable and equally dangerous, as is the post-modernist 'smorgasbord' approach to religion.[1] Both begin from the above idea that Scripture cannot have any innate overriding (and overall) authority, and extrapolate from this the seemingly logical notion that therefore it must be that we accord authority to Scripture insofar as it seems to us to merit it. If outright fundamentalism is dangerous because it puts Scripture over and against us, this way is equally dangerous because it puts us over and against Scripture. Neither way brings us into creative dialogue with Scripture. If fundamentalism pays only lip service to the concepts of human judgement and interpretation, then this approach pays only lip service to the authority of Scripture, for ironically, if we decide which pieces of Scripture are to have authority then it is in fact we who have authority over Scripture and not Scripture over us.

It should perhaps be emphasised at this stage that, as some of the other papers in this series will also be arguing, it is dangerous to make any one factor our governing one in our approach to Scripture, and this applies as much to experience and our own hermeneutical grid as it does to any other factor. All of these factors - experience, community, tradition and so on - will need to interrelate with one another and with the 'givenness' of Scripture, and with its status as revelation. It is then to the distinctive manner in which this interrelating should take place that we must next turn.

Apart from the two extreme approaches outlined above, there is further another alternative which may bring us into a real dialogue with Scripture, while fully acknowledging the ideas both of scriptural authority, and of human interpretation and judgement. Unlike the others, which tend to view Scripture as monolithic, this alternative appeals to the rich diversity of the Bible and to its multiplicity of witnesses to the ways of God.

Rather than a single authority, then, Scripture has a wide variety of *auctoritates*, as various commentators and biblical scholars have noted, among them most recently Luke Timothy Johnson in his distinguished collection of essays, *The living gospel*.[2] These may be divergent or even sometimes conflicting. All of them (individually and corporately) whilst reflecting something of the voice and authority of God, nevertheless also reflect that voice and authority as mediated, understood and interpreted through the medium of human intellect and experience. As a result this human understanding may, in equal measure sometimes illuminate and sometimes obscure the divine voice. With such a view we can, though we should not over-define the authority of Scripture, positively affirm certain aspects of authority whilst managing to steer clear of either of the two extremes we have looked at.

Thus, as we argued in the introductory paragraph, we can affirm that for Christians the Bible is reliable in its record of human/divine encounter and divine revelation and human response, and that it is, *in toto*, foundational, definitive and uniquely authoritative as the book of the Christian Church - both characterising and defining that Church. We can affirm also that it is the product of successive communities of believers, and that those individuals and communities who shaped the Bible (or who assented to the canon of Scripture as we have received it) were guided by the

Holy Spirit in their discernment. And we can affirm (the making of which affirmation profoundly relates Scripture and experience in itself) that the Word of God - as Scripture itself ultimately affirms - is not the text of Scripture, but rather the Incarnational Event, Jesus Christ, to whom the text of Scripture bears witness in different ways.

This understanding of Scripture profoundly affects how we respond. Our task is neither simply to submit to it nor to place ourselves above it, but rather to understand the processes of intellect and experience which in dialogue with God created the Scriptures, and then to ascertain as best we may, how much this witness faithfully reflects the nature and authority of God, how much of it is human interpretation (or even misinterpretation), and therefore how we respond to this witness of Scripture today. To do this we must apply our own intellect and experience to the witness of Scripture.

It should be noted that this task is a complex and ongoing one, as each generation strives afresh to relate the insights of Scripture to its own particular concerns and circumstances. Given the ever-changing nature of society and the Church - and the issues which preoccupy both - it is hardly surprising that different ages have returned different answers to the question about which aspects of Scripture are most important and relevant to them. Indeed, it may be argued that each generation may not only return different answers, but in a very real sense start afresh at the task. This generational reality was commented upon by the Danish-born philosopher Søren Kierkegaard, with regard not only to Scripture but to the whole realm of faith in his book *Fear and trembling*, published in 1843. In a passage exploring some of the difficulties of an authentic faith, for example, he says this:-

> Whatever the one generation may learn from the other, that which is genuinely human no generation learns from the foregoing. In this respect every generation begins primitively, has no different task from that of every previous generation, nor does it get further, except in so far as the preceding generation shirked its task and deluded itself. ...

> ... But the highest passion in a man is faith, and here no generation begins at any other point than did the preceding generation, every generation begins all over again, the subsequent generation gets no further than the foregoing - in so far as this remained faithful to its task and did not leave it in the lurch....[each] generation has in fact the task to perform and has nothing to do with the consideration that the foregoing generation had the same task. ...[4]

There can, then, I suggest, be no definitive and unchanging answer to the authority of Scripture, but only a succession of answers, produced by each generation in dialogue with the variety and richness of scriptural witness to God.

The effect of this is - or perhaps might most profitably be - to engender a subtle shift in just how it is that we perceive the Bible as witnessing to God. Both of the more extreme alternatives delineated earlier tend to assume (either by affirming it or by vehemently denying it) that the Bible is supposed to operate primarily as some form of divine utterance that is, through the pages of Scripture: 'God says…'. The approach advocated here implies that through the many *auctoritates* of Scripture we build up a picture not of specific utterance, but rather glimpses of the divine nature, will and purpose - as these have been seen and interpreted in very different human situations and experiences - and further, that these glimpses in turn interact creatively and robustly with our own, questioning them and in turn being questioned by them, to form part of our ongoing engagement with Scripture. The demand for this engagement (rather than any more specific criterion) is, arguably, the primary locus of scriptural authority.

Engagement and mutual questioning are essential parts of our relationship with Scripture, and have, for example, marked similarities to the relationship which the German philosopher Martin Heidegger envisaged us as having with Being. George Steiner has written extensively on Heidegger over a period of some 25 years, and articulates the quality of this Heideggerian questioning particularly deftly:

> To question truly is to enter into harmonic concordance with that which is being questioned. Far from being the initiator and sole master of the encounter…the Heideggerian asker lays himself open to that which is being questioned and becomes the vulnerable locus, the permeable space of its disclosure.

And this questioning is endless and ongoing:

> That which is 'worthy of questioning'…Is literally inexhaustible. There are no terminal answers, no last and formal decideabilities to the question of the meaning of human existence or of a Mozart sonata. … But if there can be no end to genuine questioning, the process is, none the less, not aimless. 'The wandering', says Heidegger, 'the peregrination towards that which is worthy of being questioned, is not adventure but homecoming.' Man, in his dignity, comes home to the unanswerable.[5]

As with Heidegger's 'Being', so too with Scripture: rather than us being either subject to it or set over it, the authority of Scripture consists in the demand that we be engaged with it, such that its insights, images and so on are interrogated by (and in turn themselves interrogate) our insights and glimpses of the divine. Again, as with 'Being' there is for us no final answer to our ongoing interaction with Scripture; there is only the imperative of continual return. In such a perception of and approach to Scripture there is a very clear relationship between the givenness of Scripture and our own reason and understanding. Thus the authority of Scripture emerges, in a sense, from the interplay between the two.

At first sight this may seem like casuistry, as if we are drawing some all-too-subtle distinctions, but it should be firmly emphasised that this process of attempting to understand how Scripture came to be written and to engage in dialogue with its understandings, is nowhere near the same thing as simply sitting in judgement upon it from some supposed exterior critical standpoint. The whole purpose is not to judge Scripture but to allow it to speak to us on its own terms so that our intellect and experience engage with that of scripture and tradition in an attempt to meet with the God who is witnessed to within it, discerning how faithful (or sometimes mistaken) that witness to God is, and therefore how we should respond to it today.

Finally, and again in an effort to occupy a constructive middle-ground, it should be noted that Christians wish to use the Scriptures in a wide variety of ways, some scrutinising every iota of text, and others emphasising the broad sweep of the message. As important as reaching some agreement amidst all this diversity is an acknowledgement, by all, that no group has any right either to ignore the scriptures or to demonise any other group. The scriptures are the common property of all Christians and are larger than my, your, or any of our, ways of reading them.

References:

1. Matthew 21:25b-27a (New International Version).
2. A prime example of such an approach is that afforded, in the main, by the adherents of the *Sea of Faith* network.
3. A particularly articulate recent exponent of such a position is Luke Timothy Johnson, *The living gospel* (London and New York: Continuum, 2004) pp 59-65.
4. Søren Kierkegaard, 'Fear and trembling', in *Fear and trembling and the sickness unto death* (Translated by Walter Lowrie, Princeton, New Jersey: Princeton University Press, 1941 & 1954), p.130.
5. George Steiner, *Heidegger* (Brighton: The Harvester Press, 1978) pp 57-8.

For further reading:

The following books are not strictly about Scripture, but more about our understanding of ourselves and our faith (and our retelling of scriptural stories) in a post-modern world - which will, of course, in turn, influence our approach to Scripture:
Anthony C. Thiselton, *Interpreting God and the post-modern self* (Edinburgh: T & T Clark, 1995)
Stephen Sykes, *The story of atonement* (London: DLT, 1997)
Richard Swinburne, *Revelation: from metaphor to analogy* (Oxford: Clarendon Press, 1992)
And from an earlier but equally rich Anglican perspective:
Michael Ramsey, *The Anglican spirit* (London: SPCK, 1991)

3

SCRIPTURE AND REVELATION

Maurice Elliott

BY WHAT GAUGE ought Christians to measure the requirements of faith? In practice how does God actually rule over his people, the Church? In areas of ecclesiastical dispute wherein lies the final court of arbitration? One does not need to venture very much further down the road of these and other such matters to realise that the question of authority is probably the single most important issue facing theology today. Put succinctly, it is 'the question previous to all others',[1] the one that has already been answered before a statement can be uttered or a position adopted. Claims for authority are legion, and any expression of them is at once indicative of those presuppositions which have been adopted into a particular theological system. The role of authority is crucial to the extent that as soon as it raises its head, all other issues fall by the wayside. At the risk of overstating the case, the principle of authority is ultimately the whole religious question.

It goes without saying that the exact nature of theological authority is both complex and potentially elusive. Among the various elements which must be taken into consideration are the place of God himself, the Bible, tradition, the Church, reason, conscience, the human will, emotion and faith. In view of such diversity, an acceptable starting-point is notoriously difficult. However, one useful line of approach may present itself from a brief digression into the realm of geometry.

Ordinarily, it would be tenuous to develop any significant overlap between the disciplines of theology and geometry. Nevertheless, certain shapes can be helpful in depicting theological constructs. For example, a circle speaks of mystery and that which is unknown. It exists with neither beginning nor end. It might be construed as welcoming, even all-embracing. On the other hand, a triangle is necessarily sharper. It suggests focus and purpose, and, by the inter-connectedness of its three sides, readily commends a certain expression of trinity. An even more obvious shape for Christians is that of the cross with its reminder of a call to suffering, its dual arms reaching upwards and outwards. Paul resolved to know nothing amongst the Corinthians except 'Jesus Christ and him crucified',[2] and when set against this mark of discipleship, many of the difficulties that threaten the Church are quickly seen to be of secondary importance.

The most pertinent shape for this discussion concerning authority, however, is that of a square (see Figure 1 below). If we allow that the primary emphases in any typical approach to Christian theology are on the basis of revelation, reason, tradition and experience, then each of these four sources can be plotted within such a shape. The larger square can be sub-divided, and it is the smaller sub-squares which then become determinative in the crucial matter of primacy. Before establishing how this might work in principle, however, it is necessary to explicate a little further each of the four sources under consideration.

Revelation	Reason
Tradition	Experience

FIGURE 1

The primacy of revelation

Revelation insists that all theology must begin with God. By definition, he is the supreme authority in all things, which must logically include the disclosure of himself. The study of who God is presupposes that there are aspects of both his person and his work which we can verifiably know, and so the starting point for theological investigation must be the simple fact that God has chosen to reveal himself. If we begin anywhere else than with such an insistence upon revelation, God can no longer be God, and the result of theology will be a less than satisfactory, humanly-constructed deity. Some words of the theologian Alister McGrath are apposite:

> To affirm the priority of revelation is ultimately to affirm that God is the supreme authority on God, irrespective of how humiliating this may be for self-professed human authorities on the matter. Human discourse about God is provisional, and cannot be regarded as authoritative on the basis of its own inherent credentials.[3]

Reason then is the application of rational thinking to the fact that God has chosen to disclose himself. Clearly, theology cannot function apart from the faculty to think and reflect. In terms of authority, however, the human mind cannot be elevated above that which has created it. God is not an idea to be studied or a theory to be advanced. Rather he is a person to be known, and therefore reason must be subservient to revelation, for otherwise the whole basis of theology would be undermined.

During the early centuries of the Christian era, and

even through the period of the Reformation, there was no inherent conflict in the minds of theologians as to how revelation, as they understood it, and reason might co-exist. For the Patristics, faith rested upon reason, and naturally went beyond it. In the late sixteenth century Hooker conceived of reason as being the fullness of God's natural law, which was in turn informed by, and completely consistent with, a concept of divine revelation as expressed in Scripture. With the rise of the Enlightenment, however, any such notion of God's exclusive self-revelation was rejected on the grounds of morality, primarily because it appeared unreasonable for Christian revelation not to be universal in its availability. Leading thinkers such as Kant, Lessing, Jefferson and von Harnack all began to insist upon the primacy of reason. For Enlightenment thinkers, the knowledge of God had to be universally accessible to all cultures and contexts, and consequently reason provided the only appropriate, primary resource. When set against the earlier understanding of a happy coalescence between revelation and reason, perhaps what we are really dealing with in the post-Enlightenment era is the advent of rationalism. Nevertheless, no matter how it may be finally construed for many, even to this day, reason itself has become the supreme arbiter. In such thinking, reason is permitted to stand as a completely separate authority and is considered to be the only means of liberating theology from the unnecessary constraints of an approach based upon revelation. It is precisely such an assertion which must be rejected in terms of the hermeneutical square above.

Tradition represents the accumulated wisdom and inherited custom of the Church, both catholic and local. Properly understood, it is the historical and theological legacy of the interpretation of revelation, which in turn can only ever be justified with reference to the same authoritative corpus of revelation. In other words, revelation must again remain paramount. For some, however, as with reason, tradition has become an essentially distinct authority source, especially when it is allowed to exert binding force precisely on account of its antiquity. There is an evident need for caution here. As Cyprian of Carthage once surmised: 'ancient tradition can simply be an old mistake'.[4] Clearly, no generation of believers is able to divorce itself from that which has gone before, and so there is a demand for constant reappraisal of traditional understandings, an emphasis in fact which largely triggered the Reformation.[5] For our purposes, however, what matters most is the recurring issue of primacy, and again the diagram makes for simple illustration of the crucial point. If the origin for theology were located within the sub-square of tradition, this must entail a shift away from the primacy of revelation.

Lastly, experience speaks of the need for theological thinking to impact the heart, the will and the conscience, as well as the mind. The theological task is not merely propositional or cognitive. The Christian life is about relationship and encounter with God. Theology must not only address, but also interpret and transform, both personal and indeed communal experience. Belief must determine behaviour: conduct must be informed by creed. Yet again, however, it is imperative that any acceptance of the need for genuine spiritual experience should not become the crucial, deciding factor. Were that to happen, theology would be reduced to pure subjectivity and rampant individualism. Experience has an essential role to fulfil, but it can only ever be properly construed as *explicandum* and not *explicans*.[6]

The purpose of this extended discussion is to show that, whilst there should be a proper contribution from all four sources of authority, an orthodox approach to the pursuit of theology must seek to remain firmly anchored within the sub-square of revelation. In the last analysis there can be only one final authority, and each of reason, tradition and experience must therefore bow before revelation. Such a thesis is the only acceptable genesis for Christian thinking. The other three sources are essential for experiential fullness as well as academic rigour. Without doubt revelation would be completely meaningless were it not for the application of reason. Similarly any notion of experience is largely dependent upon the particularity of cultural or denominational tradition. For healthy discipleship there is an obvious and natural place for reason, tradition and experience, not least for the manner in which they themselves are inter-related, and indeed for a lesser sense whereby God can choose at times to clarify aspects of his will in precisely these ways. Nevertheless, it is the issue of primacy which remains paramount. Whereas revelation can and must interact with each of reason, tradition and experience, in terms of ultimate authority these other sources are of secondary significance.

The premise hereby established is a matter of both faith and logic. Logic insists that the nature of the theological task requires the Godhead to reveal himself. Faith believes that he has, in fact, done precisely that. If this premise is accepted, the next challenge must be to establish a normative basis for the Christian understanding of revelation.

The Christian understanding of revelation

In general terms God has revealed himself through creation and conscience. Humanity has common access to the nature of God's character by virtue of the natural world with all its diversity and intricacy. Equally there exist certain innate, yet universally agreed, standards of behaviour. Generally speaking, murder is murder, theft is theft, and there are admissible norms of truth and falsehood, for example. For Christians, however, the more pressing demand is for recognition of the principle of special revelation. According to this, it is asserted that God has revealed himself in three persons over the course of salvation history culminating in the incarnation of Jesus Christ, to all of which Holy Scripture is customarily viewed as the authoritative witness. For the health and well-being of the Church, therefore, it begins to become apparent that, because the scriptures have thus recorded the content of God's self-revelation, it is essential to submit to their primary authority, or, to be more precise, to believe in God's authority as thereby exercised through the scriptures.

This thesis will naturally require much fuller clarification. Before addressing this, however, it is worth noting that such an affirmation mirrors the received doctrinal position of all the major Western Christian denominations. For example, an agreed statement of the various Lutheran Churches posits:

> We believe, teach and confess that the prophetic and apostolic writings of the Old and New Testaments are the only rule and norm according to which all doctrines must be appraised and judged. Other writings of ancient and modern teachers must be subordinated to the Scriptures and should be received no further than as witnesses to the fashion in which the doctrine of the prophets and apostles was preserved in post-apostolic times.[7]

Again, from the Westminster Confession,[8] which is foundational to the Reformed and Presbyterian Churches we read:

> Although the light of nature, and the works of creation and providence, do so far manifest the goodness, wisdom, and power of God, as to leave men inexcusable; yet they are not sufficient to give that knowledge of God which is necessary for salvation; therefore it pleased the Lord, at sundry times, and in divers manners, to reveal himself...and afterwards to commit the same wholly unto writing; which maketh the holy Scripture most necessary...The authority of the holy scripture, for which it ought to be believed and obeyed, dependeth not upon the testimony of any man or church, but wholly upon God.[9]

As from the Second Vatican Council, the official position of the Roman Catholic Church, also affirms the uniquely authoritative role of Holy Scripture:

> In his goodness and wisdom God chose to reveal himself

and to make known to us the hidden purpose of his will... Jesus perfected revelation by fulfilling it through his words and deeds, his signs and wonders, but especially through his death and glorious resurrection...God has seen to it that what he had revealed for the salvation of all nations would abide perpetually in its full integrity and be handed on to all generations. Therefore he commissioned the apostles to preach...and the commission was fulfilled also by those apostles and apostolic men who under the inspiration of the Holy Spirit committed the message of salvation to writing.[10]

Most pertinent of all, the received position of Anglicanism is entirely indicative of submission to the primacy of scriptural authority, as has recently been reaffirmed in the Virginia Report:

Anglicans affirm the sovereign authority of the Holy Scriptures as the medium through which God by the Spirit communicates his word in the Church and thus enables people to respond with understanding and faith. The Scriptures are a uniquely inspired witness to the divine revelation, and the primary norm for Christian faith and life.[11]

The report goes on to develop the specifically Anglican understanding of Scripture, reason and tradition, but even within this schema, primacy is clearly and rightly afforded to the Bible.

Given, therefore, that all shades of institutional Western Christianity proclaim scriptural authority, the key issue must now be to address the basis of such a viewpoint. What gives the Bible - this collection of very varied, ancient texts - a right to impose its teaching on the thinking of the Church in every age? In what sense are its contents timeless? What also can be said about the matter of interpretation, for sometimes even those who accept the authority of the Bible have arrived at very different conclusions as to its meaning? It is to these and other such questions that we now turn.

The duality of Scripture

Every time an Anglican congregation listens to a reading from the Bible, the liturgical response is typically: ' "This is the Word of the Lord" (minister). "Thanks be to God" (people)'. In pronouncing these words, the believers rehearse a profound truth. In effect they are declaring that the scriptures are more than simply human writings. The words they contain are in fact the very words of God himself. Enshrined within them *per se*, and in the witness that they offer, is a divine voice that has somehow resulted in what is known and acknowledged to be the Word of God. Out of this vein emerges the traditional understanding of God's self-revelation as embodied in Scripture, and further, it is this divine nature of the biblical text which thus guarantees its permanent authority:

> The authority of Scripture means that all the words in

Scripture are God's words in such a way that to disbelieve or disobey any word of Scripture is to disbelieve or disobey God.[12]

To say that these words are divine, however, is in no sense to deny that they are also human in their origin. Of course it was necessary for Paul and James and John to write their epistles whether themselves or by amanuensis. Similarly, Luke and the other evangelists carefully investigated all the matters concerning Jesus. In the psalms, David and others speak eloquently of what had been their own personal experience. In other Old Testament writings, scribes and prophets interpret the unfolding events of both current affairs and history. Yet simultaneously, behind such human words, which were thus recorded as human Scriptures, these texts are uniquely authoritative in the life and mission of the Church for the simple reason that they are considered also to be God's words. Out of them God's purpose and his will are directly disclosed.

The net effect of what Christians have traditionally believed, therefore, is that in the 66 books of the Bible there is a duality of natures, and for an appreciation of scriptural authority this point cannot be over-emphasised. As theologian John Stott has put it:

> God-breathed is not the only account which Scripture gives of itself, since God's mouth was not the only mouth

involved in its production. The same Scripture which says "the mouth of the Lord has spoken" also says that God spoke "by the mouth of his holy prophets". Out of whose mouth did Scripture come, then? God's or man's? The only biblical answer is both.[13]

The Scriptures are both human and divine. They are in the same moment historical and timeless, finite and eternal. Such an antinomy is perhaps alien to modern ears and a post-Enlightenment mindset. Nevertheless it perhaps becomes more appreciable when set alongside the Church's received Christological understanding of Jesus himself. To the eye of faith, Christ is at the same time the Son of man and the Son of God. He is fully both, and only as such has Christian theology been able to maintain its integrity, doing justice to that which is properly believed. In fact it is demonstrable that the majority of Christological heresies have taken root precisely when one of these aspects has been over-emphasised to the detriment of the other:

> Just as in the person of Christ we must neither affirm his deity in such a way as to deny his humanity, nor affirm his humanity in such a way as to deny his deity, but rather affirm both equally, refusing to allow either to contradict the other, so in our doctrine of Scripture we must neither affirm that it is the Word of God in such a way as to deny that it is the word of human beings (which is fundamentalism), nor affirm that it is the words of human beings in such a way as to deny that it is the Word of God (which is liberalism), but rather affirm both equally, refusing to allow either to contradict the other.[14]

Returning to the doctrine of revelation, it might be postulated that much of the contemporary crisis with regard to scriptural authority has resulted from the manner in which a wedge has been driven between these two crucial aspects of the revealed text, namely its divinity and its humanity. One is tempted to adjure, albeit significantly out of context: 'What God hath joined together, let not man put asunder'.[15]

The inspiration of the canon

Holy Scripture has definitive authority in that, by dint of a dual nature, it conveys both the words of men and, more crucially, the Word of God. To put it another way, through the word of the scriptures, God has disclosed himself and is therefore able to exercise his dominion in the life of the Church. This is what is meant by scriptural authority, and the proposition underlying it depends further upon the concomitant doctrines of inspiration and canonicity.

By the providence of God, through the outworking of human agencies, the texts of Holy Scripture have been preserved for posterity. The process by which this resulted in the Bible as we now possess it naturally involved matters of selectivity, and such selection, under the guidance of the Holy Spirit, was consistently believed to be made on the basis of that which, in the mind of the faith community, was considered to be inspired. It is no coincidence therefore that the scriptures attest their own inspired quality. As Paul wrote to Timothy:

> All Scripture is God-breathed and is useful for teaching, correcting and training in righteousness so that the person of God may be thoroughly equipped for every good work.[16]

In the first instance this clearly refers to the Hebrew Scriptures as they had come to be received within first-century Judaism, and in many cases the origin of such a sense of inspiration or 'God-breathed-ness' is not difficult to identify. The earliest warrant of inspiration came when Moses recorded that which the Lord disclosed to him in the form of the Ten Commandments.[17] Again, on numerous occasions the oft-repeated cries of the Old Testament prophets were: 'The word of the Lord came to me'. 'Thus saith the Lord'.[18] These seers proclaimed, and then recorded, that which was given to them by the inner moving of the Holy Spirit. Turning to the Christian writings, and in particular to the gospels, this notion of inspired words derived directly from the principle of the incarnation. Since Jesus was believed to be the spirit-filled Messiah, his own words were considered to be inspired, and, following from this, a vibrant tradition of oral and apostolic transmission then enabled the Church to recognise the authenticity of these words.

Alongside these more overt examples, however, there is for Christian people a sense whereby all the books in what have come to be received as the Old and New Testaments are divinely inspired. For example, in the words of Peter referring to the prophets: 'men spoke as they were carried along by the Holy Spirit'.[19] This aspect of inspiration may be more oblique and difficult to explain, but in the nature of faith it is the only ultimately persuasive reason for fully submitting to the authority of God as mediated through the Bible.

As already suggested, the primary test of inspiration was quite simply the role and reception of such Scriptures at the centre of the communal life of faith, and in this regard there is much evidence to support the traditionally held views of both the Old and New Testament canons. For example, the latest of the Hebrew canonical books are Malachi, Ezra and Nehemiah. In the period following these, namely from the early fifth century BC, it was generally understood amongst the people of Israel that no further authoritative words had been given by the Lord. This is repeatedly attested in a number of sources such as the inter-testamental work, 1 Maccabees, the history of

Josephus as well as other Rabbinnic literature.[20] Any writings dated during this later period, therefore, were not accepted as having equal authority with the rest of the scriptures and hence were not included as part of the canon. Again it is more than a little significant that whereas Jesus and the other New Testament authors quote almost 300 passages of the Hebrew scriptures as divinely authoritative, they never once cite these later apocryphal texts. Thus, it is demonstrable that the Old Testament canon was already well-established and substantially settled by the time of the first century.

With regard to the New Testament, it is revealing to observe the self-conscious awareness of the apostles about their own divinely appointed role. Addressing the Corinthians and the Thessalonians, for example, Paul explicitly claimed that much of his teaching was inspired by revelation from God.[21] More subtly, in his first letter to Timothy he quite deliberately implied his own authority to be equivalent with that of Moses.[22] From the very inception of the Christian era it is essential to realise that the seal of inspiration was placed upon even some of the earliest extant New Testament documents. In his second epistle Peter accorded to the writings of Paul the status of scriptural authority.[23] Likewise Paul in writing to Timothy takes a saying from the lips of Jesus and quite intentionally sets it alongside an already accepted and authoritative Scripture from the Old Testament.[24]

The Christian canon may have taken some centuries before it was finally formalised and clearly the process involved difficult, hotly contested decisions at a human level. Nevertheless, it is again clear that the primary test for all those documents in circulation during the life of the early post-apostolic church was quite simply their accuracy in recording the words and deeds of Christ himself, and their proven origin with Christ's own appointed delegates - the apostles. Following from this, under the sovereign directing of God himself, the simple process by which canonical decisions were taken was a recognition of how each text was perceived to be instructive not only for a local situation, but also for the preservation of the whole community of faith.

Having said all of that, there can be no argument in favour of an automatic, mechanical process of inspiration. A conservative understanding of the doctrine of divine inspiration differs markedly from the more fundamentalist, and ultimately anti-intellectual, notion of Holy Scripture having been dictated verbatim by God. As noted above, the insistence upon a duality of natures allows for both the Scriptures as the Word of God on the one hand, and the Scriptures as a free composition of human authors on the other. In turn such duality permits the biblical text to encompass its rich diversity of style, with letters and law-books, poetic literature and lament, history and apocalyptic. Moreover it demands that all the Scriptures can and should be exposed to the full rigours of critical investigation. By dint of their human nature, they merit no less than this for the sake of cogency. By virtue of their divine attribute, they can never be undone and are more than able to withstand the full weight of theological criticism, be it literary, redaction, source, cultural or textual in its character. Most crucially of all, it bears repetition at this juncture that what Christians properly believe is not the authority of a collection of books *per se*. Much rather they willingly submit to the authority of God as mediated through the revelatory nature of the Scriptures, and supremely (as we shall see later) they do this out of reverence for Christ.

At this point a rational view will readily observe that there are of course a number of difficulties and even apparent contradictions within the overall canon of Holy Scripture, and not least even within the New Testament itself. In the aspect of its humanity there can of course be difficulties in understanding the

Bible, and Christian people are by no means oblivious to these. Nevertheless, a prior acceptance of the primacy of revelation, allied to a properly submissive attitude, will want to insist that it is infinitely preferable to see such problems, not as insuperable and therefore as a reason to reject or question scriptural authority, but rather as being as yet unresolved. This has to be the only logical outworking of the primacy of revelation. To put it in a slightly different way, a fully-rounded biblical theology will maintain that even those verses that may appear obscure or outrageous should only be properly interpreted in the context of the entire canon. The fact that there are certain problem passages need not therefore diminish either the divine inspiration of Scripture as a whole, or indeed its ultimate authority. Furthermore, there can be a danger of imposing upon the scriptural texts the wrong kind of expectation. Clearly the early apostolic writers did not all say exactly the same thing. Yet again it can be contended in response that such diversity need not inevitably require the conclusion that the overall message is flatly contradictory. Some words of N.T. Wright are helpful here:

> Just because some Western theologians cannot see how [certain New Testament categories] fit coherently together does not mean that they did not in the first century. A good many well-known apparent problems of inner-canonical coherence are of this type. Those that remain are best seen as a

challenge to further thought rather than as an undermining of the remarkably consistent proclamation of the New Testament.[25]

In many instances the passage of time and the advance of academic insight have already contributed towards clarifying many issues which may have been problematic to past generations. There is every reason, therefore, to believe and expect that in the future this may again prove to be the case.

Jesus and Scripture

In the final analysis, Christianity is a personal religion. It is not solely concerned with the reading of a book. Instead, it has to do with the unique revelation of God in the historical figure who stands at its very centre, namely Jesus Christ. As Wright has stated: 'the historical figure of Jesus of Nazareth is the criterion by which every Christian affirmation has to be judged, and in the light of which it stands or falls'.[26]

In view of this, the first, perhaps rather obvious point is that outside Scripture there could be no reliable knowledge of this Jesus figure. Not only is this so, but in addition, when we begin to investigate the actual message of the Bible, it becomes clear that the same Jesus is the only key to its proper interpretation. It is true to say that in every sense he brings Scripture to its climax. To adopt some words of von Allmen:

> Jesus Christ is the centre of the biblical revelation since it bears witness to him. He is both the heart (what sums it up and makes it live) and the head (what explains and justifies it). To read the Bible without meeting him is to read it badly, to preach the Bible without proclaiming him is to preach it falsely.[27]

There is thus an intimate connection between the word of God incarnate and the word of God in Scripture, and certainly Jesus himself seems to have been fully aware of this vital link. For example, on the road to Emmaus we read of how 'beginning with Moses and all the prophets, he explained to [the two disciples] what was said in all the Scriptures concerning *himself*.[28] Not only therefore does the Bible lead us to Christ; the reverse is also true in that Christ then leads us to the Bible.

In the minds of Christian people, Jesus embodies the contours of the redeemed life. As such it cannot be ignored that the attitude of Jesus himself gives further persuasive evidence of the need for submission to scriptural primacy. The gospels disclose him as someone who fully accepted the authority of the Hebrew canon. For him the texts of the 'Old Testament' were not merely an historical record, but rather the true and living word of the true and living God. In every aspect of his own life and ministry, therefore, Jesus portrayed the need for Scripture to remain central. During his temptation by the devil he resorted on three occasions to the text of Deuteronomy, voicing its authority in the words: 'It is written…'.[29] In matters of morality he often asked: 'Have you not read? What does the Scripture say?...'.[30] He was constantly aware of the need for the prophecy of Hebrew writings to be fulfilled, and perhaps the most telling instance of this were his words uttered during his final agony in the Garden of Gethsemane.

Do you think I cannot call on my Father, and he will at once put at my disposal more than twelve legions of angels? *But how then would the Scriptures be fulfilled that say it must happen in this way?* [31]

Jesus evidently felt himself constrained by the need for personal obedience to what the Scriptures said, even to the point of accepting death on the cross for that very reason. Furthermore, he repeatedly emphasised his desire not to abolish the law but rather to complete it:

> Do not think that I have come to abolish the Law or the Prophets; I have come not to abolish them but to fulfil them. I tell you the truth, until heaven and earth disappear, not the

smallest letter, not the least stroke of a pen, will by any means disappear from the Law until everything is accomplished.[32]

These words from the Sermon on the Mount are followed directly by a series of six antitheses in which Jesus seeks not to contradict the law, but to correct contemporary misinterpretations of what it said. The determination in his mind was to demonstrate the unchanging nature and relevance of that which God had revealed. For him 'the Scripture [could] not be broken'.[33]

In view of this, it is not surprising to infer that Jesus clearly envisaged that his teaching, given both publicly and on numerous occasions more privately to his disciples, was something that would also be written down and preserved for the benefit of the Church in future generations: 'The Counsellor, the Holy Spirit, whom the Father will send in my name, will teach you all things and will remind you of everything I have said to you'.[34]

The underlying notion was that these new scriptures of Christ's designated apostles would come to exercise a similar authority in the new community of faith, as had the texts of the Hebrew canon for his own and previous generations. We have already seen how in practice this came to be the case.

For Christians, therefore, the desire for, and importance of, submission to scriptural authority is nothing more than a reflection of the desire for, and importance of, submission to the lordship of Jesus himself. He is the object of their worship, which expresses itself in humble submission, and at the same time he is the pattern of their discipleship.

The interpretation of Scripture

What then finally can be said of those principles that are necessary for a proper interpretation of Scripture? More than anything else, it is with regard to the meaning of the scriptures that differences tend to emerge even between those who ostensibly profess to accept the authority of the Bible in the first place. Again the hermeneutical square with which this discussion began is helpful, for in the last analysis the interpretation of the text is always substantially determined by those presuppositions which are brought to it.

Hence, for example, if my experience is to be the deciding factor, I shall want hear from Scripture only those truths which edify me, and will tend correspondingly to abrogate or explain away anything which stands against my own personal sense of well-being and fulfilment. Again, and herein certain aspects of Roman Catholic doctrine and indeed the more recent documents of the Anglican-Roman Catholic International Commission (ARCIC) are a case in point, should tradition become the overriding principle, then it becomes impossible for Scripture to search and to counter those teachings of the Church that have already become established through the course of history. Were reason to be accepted as the supreme court of arbitration, that would allow for new insights continually and completely undermine the received wisdom of the faith. It would become impossible to know that in any sense we are in possession of the truth, for future years may yield up some, as yet undiscovered, knowledge to the detriment of all that is accepted in the present. And so we are brought back again logically to the primacy of revelation which insists that the biblical canon as a whole is both coherent and complete.

With regard to the matter of interpretation, an emphasis on revelation will want to assert further that the Scriptures as we have them now, and not least in view of the attitude of Jesus towards them, are sufficient. Since God is the one who has inspired the scriptures to be written, and left us with the living witness of his own Son, it is entirely reasonable to suppose that he also continues to lead the Church, by the Spirit, into a proper understanding of how they should be understood and explained. Equally, since the basis of this belief is the fact that he has chosen to disclose himself and his divine will in the first place, faith-based logic decrees that he has left us with all that we need to know for life and godliness. The message of the Scriptures is completely sufficient, or in the words of the sixth Article of the 39 Articles of Religion: 'they contain all things necessary to salvation'.[35]

Finally, there can be no denying of the fact that the Scriptures are, in a word of the reformers, perspicuous. That is to say, they are clear in their essential meaning, not least with regard to their central message. Of course this is not to deny that the interpretation of the same Scriptures can prove complex. Even Peter, commenting on the writings of his fellow apostle Paul, noted that there were certain things which were difficult to understand.[36] The perspicuity of the text applies to its central message and for that very reason the core teaching of the Scriptures can be understood by all without exception. All of the reformers bore testimony to this crucial understanding, and perhaps some words of Thomas Cranmer, seen by many as a key founding father of Anglicanism, may suffice to make the point:

> [Holy Scripture] ... containeth fruitful instruction and erudition for every man; if any things be necessary to be learned, of the holy Scripture we learn it... . Here may all manner of persons, men, women, young, old, learned, unlearned, rich, poor, priests, laymen, lords, ladies, officers, tenants, and mean men, virgins, wives, widows, lawyers, merchants, artificers, husbandmen, all manner of persons, of what estate or condition soever they may be, in this book learn all things what they ought to believe, what they ought to do, and what they should not do, as well concerning Almighty God, as also concerning themselves and all other.[37]

Conclusion

A conservative approach to the meaning of scriptural authority rests squarely upon the doctrine of revelation. It does not deny that there is a proper place for the application of reason, the benefit of tradition and the outcome of experience. Each of these approaches has much to contribute in the pursuit of fullness for academic theology. Nevertheless, primacy must remain at all times with the notion that God can only be known on the basis of how he has determined to reveal himself. In turn this presupposes that the text of the Bible, as it was originally given, is directly inspired by God through his Holy Spirit. This is not to suggest that he dictated it or that human authors were by-passed. Rather it must be understood within a sense of dual nature, and this duality is further reflected in the process by which the scriptural canon came together in the first place. When it comes to the interpretation of Holy Scripture, the key determining factors must be an appreciation of biblical theology in its fullest sense and a proper reverence for the person and work of Jesus Christ. According to Christological persuasion, disciples in every age have sought to follow the example of their Lord. The questions they want to ask, therefore, concern how he himself received, expanded, interpreted and applied the scriptures.

This approach remains the cherished position of a substantial proportion of sincere Christian people. In particular, for evangelical Christians, who adhere utterly to this perspective, there is a contention that the weight of history and tradition favours this particular line of interpretation for biblical authority. If this is so, then it also follows that the source of those matters which are currently innovative must lie elsewhere. Such an approach to the Bible cannot, and does not, claim to have every answer to those issues which continue to threaten the very existence of the institutional Church. Furthermore, those who espouse such an approach to biblical authority would distance themselves significantly from any outright expression of fundamentalism. In the last analysis, however, the absolute and primary authority of God as exercised through Holy Scripture must be a *sine qua non* for the well-being of the Church in this and every age.

Given that the scriptures do continue to reveal the nature and character of God, and in that sense their message is a living word, it means most of all their story of salvation is as yet unfinished. Christian people in every age have the privilege, not only of knowing that which has gone before in the foundation of the faith and indeed the very mind of Jesus who stands as the head of the Church, but in actual reality of becoming participants themselves.

The divine drama calls forth new actors in each succeeding generation, and in view of that, it is perhaps apposite to give the final word to a short extract from Deuter-onomy wherein the Lord himself is heard to sound an important note of caution: 'See that you do all I command you; do not add to it or take away from it'.[38]

The original words bore reference to the revelation which God gave to Moses. The principle is one which the Church of today would do well to observe.

References:

1. R.C. Johnson, quoted in Sinclair B. Ferguson and David F. Wright (eds.), *New dictionary of theology* (Leicester: IVP, 1988), p. 64.
2. 1 Corinthians 2:2.
3. Alister E.McGrath, *A passion for truth. The intellectual coherence of evangelicalism* (Leicester: Apollos, 1996) p. 3.
4. *ibid.*, p. 95.
5. *ecclesia semper reformanda* was a well-worn slogan of all the magisterial reformers.
6. In other words, as 'that which must be explained' as opposed to 'that which gives the explanation'. See McGrath, *A passion for truth, op. cit.*, p. 78.
7. 'The doctrine of holy Scripture in the Lutheran Confessions - an anthology', in T.G. Tappert (ed.), *The book of concord: the confessions of the Evangelical Lutheran Church* (Philadelphia: Fortress Press, 1959), p. 2.
8. During the Reformation, numerous Confessions of Faith were published. The Westminster Confession, dating from 1646, is a systematic exposition of high Calvinism, the vows of which form the doctrinal touchstone of most Presbyterian, Congregationalist and even Baptist Churches.
9. A. McPherson (ed.), *The Westminster Confession of Faith* (Glasgow: Eccles Printers, 1985), p.19.
10. The difficulty for Roman Catholicism remains its insistence on the magisterium, or teaching authority, of the Church. In terms of the hermeneutical square (see figure 1, page 69 above) its position is more likely to straddle the two sub-squares of revelation and tradition. See *Dogmatic constitution on divine revelation Dei Verbum solemnly promulgated by His Holiness Pope Paul VI on November 18, 1965*, website documents of the Second Vatican Council, p.3, www.vatican.va
11. 'The Virginia Report: the report of the Inter-Anglican Theological and Doctrinal Commission', in *The Official Report of the Lambeth Conference 1998* (Harisburg, Pennsylvania: ACC, 1999), p.32.
12. W. Grudem, *Systematic theology* (Michigan: IVP, 1994), p.81.
13. J.R.W. Stott, *The contemporary Christian* (Leicester: Inter-Varsity

Press,1992), p.168.
14. *ibid.*, p. 168.
15. Matthew 19:6.
16. 2 Timothy 3:16-17.
17. Exodus 20.
18. For example, Isaiah 8:1, Jeremiah 1:4, Ezekiel 2:1, Hosea 1:1, Joel 1:1, etc.
19. 2 Peter 1:21
20. The writer of 1 Maccabees speaks of a great distress 'such as had not been since the time that prophets ceased to appear among the people' (1 Maccabees 9:27). Likewise Josephus in *Against Apion* 1:41 observes that 'from Artaxerxes to our own times a complete history has been written, but has not been deemed worthy of equal credit with the earlier records, because of the failure of the exact succession of the prophets'. The *Babylonian talmud* of the Rabbinic tradition asserts that 'after the latter prophets Haggai, Zechariah and Malachi had died, the Holy Spirit departed from Israel'.
21. See for example 1 Corinthians 7:10ff: 'To the married I give this command (not I, but the Lord).... To the rest I say this (I, not the Lord)...'. See also 1 Thessalonians 2:13: '...when you received the word of God, which you heard from us, you accepted it not as the word of men, but as it actually is, the word of God'. In differentiating the levels of his teaching, Paul nonetheless affirms that much of it was given to him by direct revelation. In fact, his whole argument in Galatians is premised upon the claim that the gospel he preached 'is not something that man made up', but rather that he had 'received it by revelation from Jesus Christ' (Galatians 1:11-12).
22. In 2 Timothy 3, Paul deliberately sets up a comparison between the opposition which Jannes and Jambres maintained against Moses in Exodus and the way in which certain false teachers within the Ephesian churches were standing against him. The implication, therefore, is that he considers his own rank of authority amongst the people of God to equate with that of the patriarch.

23. '[Paul's] letters contain some things that are hard to understand, which ignorant and unstable people distort, as they do the other scriptures', see 2 Peter 3:16.
24. See 1 Timothy 5:18. The first quotation is from Deuteronomy 25:4 and was therefore an already accepted scripture. The rest of the verse which forms a continuum occurs not in the Old Testament, but rather is found in Luke 10:7.
25. N.T. Wright, *Scripture and the authority of God* (London: SPCK, 2005), p.39.
26. *ibid.*, p.31.
27. Quoted in Stott, *The contemporary Christian, op. cit.*, p.167.
28. Luke 24:27.
29. Matthew 4:1-11.
30. For example Matthew 19:4.
31. Matthew 26:53-54.
32. Matthew 5:17-18.
33. John 10:35.
34. John 14:26.
35. *The Book of Common Prayer* (Dublin: Columba Press, 2004), p.779.
36. 2 Peter 3:16.
37. 'A prologue or preface made by the Most Reverend Father in God, Thomas, Archbishop of Canterbury', quoted in John Edmund Cox (ed.), *Miscellaneous writings and letters of archbishop Cranmer*, edited for the Parker Society (Cambridge: The University Press, 1846), p. 121.
38. Deuteronomy 12:32.

For further reading:

D.L. Edwards & J.R.W. Stott, *Essentials: a liberal-evangelical dialogue* (London: Hodder, 1988)
G. Goldsworthy, *Preaching the whole Bible as Christian Scripture* (Leicester: Eerdmans, 2000)
W. Grudem, *Systematic theology* (Michigan: IVP, 1994), especially chapters 2-8
D. Jackman, *I believe in the Bible* (London: Hodder, 2000)

Alister E. McGrath, *A passion for truth. The intellectual coherence of evangelicalism* (Leicester: Apollos, 1996)

N.T. Wright, *Scripture and the authority of God* (London: SPCK, 2005)

4

SCRIPTURE AND COMMUNITY

Sue Patterson

IN HIS ESSAY 'Scripture, consensus and community', George Lindbeck describes the relationship between Scripture and community (or Church) as one of mutual interpretation.[1] This is a statement to which we might all want to respond: 'yes, yes indeed that is true.' Yet to talk of Scripture and community immediately begs the question: which community - the Christian community, or the wider community (or both)? And in any case, what do we mean by 'community'? For to take on board such a statement requires us not only to acknowledge the incredible diversity of Christian community and question the criteria of community to which Christians assent and by which they live, but to consider the degree to which both the Christian community at large and individual Christian communities live up to what might be said to be the ideal of Christian community.

In part one of what follows, I will examine these questions. Then in part two, having complicated everything as far as a paper like this will allow, I will address the relationship of Scripture and community and draw out some practical implications.

Human community and Christian community

The word, 'community' literally means 'with unity' or 'unity with'. A community is a group of people who live in unity with each other. Communities will differ according to the nature or source of that unity - for example, whether blood relationship, ethnic group, physical proximity, or common cause or need, also whether a geographical or 'gathered' unit, (and whether, in that case, a historical or newly formed entity) - and according to the way that unity is maintained and ordered. As we know, even the smallest, simplest communities operate according to rules or laws, implicit or explicit, for the survival and mutual support and benefit of their members both individually and together, and all communities have leaders and ways of appointing leaders, whether this process is formally acknowledged or not.

If we play at being sociologists and look at Christian community in terms of what constitutes human community, we will consider it as a type or species of human community. This analysis may be quite limited in Christian terms, as its evaluation of the successfulness or otherwise of a community is likely to be restricted to its degree of cohesiveness and extent to which it allows and promotes human flourishing.

Nevertheless, a consideration of Christian community at this level does, importantly, recognise that human community is 'natural'. Depending on one's viewpoint, as human beings we have evolved, or have been designed, to live in community. It has been empirically demonstrated that our ability to develop to our full potential physically, mentally and spiritually depends upon our being born into and raised within communities in which we have a meaningful place and role, and where we are accepted, loved, taught, and encouraged.

Thus, on these sociological grounds, there are good and bad communities as well as successful and unsuccessful ones. A community may, for example, be strongly united (cohesive) but through the repressive regime of a dictatorial leader or family dynasty. Such a community will undermine and eventually destroy the true welfare and happiness of its members, and so scores negatively on human flourishing. More subtly, a strongly cohesive 'tribal' community may effectively ensure its survival and the survival of its members, but promote an insularity and exclusiveness which in the end will undermine the flourishing of its members through restriction of experience and promotion of fear and prejudice. On the other hand, a community which lacks cohesion will sooner or later simply cease to exist, however great its attempts to promote human flourishing; and thus, in the end, it will not succeed in that either.

Already, by stating things in this way, implicitly the fact of human community has been drawn inside a Christian understanding of community as interpreted by Scripture, as a God-ordained and revealed aspect of creation. Such an aspect has potential to provide both the best and worst arrangements for human living; and so, in the light of the latter, community under the law, is judged sinful, in need of redemption.

Of course, an adequate drawing inside a Christian understanding would regard human community as redeemed in Christ, to the extent that it is accepting of that redemption. But at this stage I propose to use this basic drawing-inside as the framework for looking again at the relationship between human community and Christian community in particular, and then, as integral with that relationship, at the relationship between Christian community and the wider culture.

Christian community - which for present purposes I take to be a community of people who define themselves as Christian, such as a local church or parish - shares all the virtues and vices of human community in general. In more specifically theological terms, it is both a repository of the goodness of Creation and a participator in a 'fallenness' which may present as a disunity pretending to be unity ('living the lie' of community); or as coerced or imprisoned community (dictatorship); or as a tribalism in which unity and communal identity are defined and protected through opposition and exclusion ('We don't have candles because we are not Roman Catholics').

As such, Christian community, like any other community, is a product of its history, geography, socio-politico-economic circumstances and needs. Formed by all of these, its self-definition gives rise to, shapes, maintains, and perpetuates, the rules by which it lives, which are generally rules that are lived and passed on by example, rather than specifically articulated. The historical continuity of community is like a stone wall repaired on so many occasions that some might say it is no longer the same wall. Yet it is, because of its continuity of existence over time.

CASE STUDY 1

When I walked into the small neat church just south of the border to take the Christmas Eve communion service, the first thing I noticed was the two Union Jacks mounted on the wall to the side of the chancel. 'Why do you have Union Jacks on your wall?', I inquired of one of the wardens. 'They've always been there,' he replied.

At the same time, of course, Christian community subscribes, or professes to subscribe, to another set of rules for living as stated in Scripture. These rules, whether they are understood in terms of law or gospel will invariably clash with some, or even all, of the lived rules of the 'natural' and 'fallen' Christian community. Here repentance involves a self-critical awareness of the presence of the 'natural', implicit 'law of the community'. To what extent is this hidden factor of unity calling the shots in its practices and therefore operating to a degree as an undermining sub-text in its belief structure?

The local community and the wider culture

The Christian community's uneasy double-life is a living out of a particular relationship between Christian beliefs, values and practices, and those of the wider community in which it lives and moves and has its being, where that wider culture consists of a blend of the religious and the secular, and where the religious element includes both other Christian communities and those of other faiths. The relationships between the beliefs, values and practices of a particular Christian community and those of the surrounding culture may take various forms: they may be harmonious, discontinuous, compartmentalised, or conflicting to varying degrees; or they may display all of these characteristics at one time or another, depending on what is going on in the community or the culture. Yet, as we know all too well, where or when there is conflict, the Church community will not always be right, but may be guilty of 'pharisaism', judgmental harshness, intolerance, or inhospitality - it is not simply a matter of 'good Church and evil world'! Nor is discontinuity or compartmentalization to be taken as a sure sign of moral schizophrenia or hypocrisy, conscious or otherwise. As I have suggested, the meeting-place of good and bad, redeemed and unredeemed, is within the Christian community itself.

As a result of their sheer insistence and pervasiveness, it is easy to confuse commonly held secular notions of community with Christian ones, to the point of holding that the former values are indistinguishable from Christian ones. Many people unthinkingly subscribe to the fallacy that what is familiar and prevalent, and therefore must be lived with, must accordingly be right, or at least acceptable ('Sure, that's just the game of rugby', said a parishioner, when challenged about gratuitous violence on the field). Secular notions of what constitutes the acceptable community may insidiously squeeze the Christian community into their mould.

CASE STUDY 2

A New Zealand city parish sees its main purpose (and justification for its being taken seriously by a very secular wider culture) as being a provider of a social service: to fund-raise for charity through its 'opportunity shop'. What began as a mission venture has become indistinguishable from the work done by secular agencies. There appears to be little connection between the worshipping life of the Church and this all-consuming activity.

Of course, the reverse is required if priority is to be given to Christian values, and Christian community is to retain its distinctiveness from the surrounding culture. The requirement is that the lived facts of life in the wider community be assimilated (either positively of negatively) into the Scripture-framed world of Christian belief and practice allowing that openness to these realities will inevitably modify these beliefs, but trusting that through this process the Holy Spirit may lead the community into new interpretations that open up the Scriptures further.[2]

Culture and communal particularity

Arguably, then, Christian community is both of the culture and counter-cultural in being radically assimilative while retaining its distinctive identity. I have already mentioned the incredible diversity of Christian community: the many-faceted body that is the Church is a mosaic of multi-stranded local particularities formed through the interactions of personalities, culture, history, and geography. We see this diversity to a startling degree without leaving the shores of this island. Again, this diversity, or particularity, is built into the nature of human community. In any community each member sees things from a slightly different perspective, and the whole community together will have a joint perspective, vision, or self-understanding, which is both a composite of some or all of its members' viewpoints, and something that is different from all of them. The community itself has an identity, a 'mind', as it were, formed from the sum of the histories, circumstances and personalities of its members, combined with its own history, circumstances and particular location.

Mobility is another factor that relates both to our knowledge of our history and to our having left home. We are all temporally mobile within our culture or tradition, although we will differ in how wide or narrow our knowledge of this grounding is. Not all of us have been spatially mobile, in having left the locality of our birth and attempted to live in another one. Those who have been are able to acquire a double-sided view of their own culture, from within and from outside. They are aware that wherever they happen to stand in the world, whatever beliefs they profess and practices they engage in, there are other ways of seeing and doing things, other perspectives on reality.

These factors mean that each community views reality through a particular framework and interprets that reality differently from other communities. As a result, each community will have a slightly different sense of community and purpose, and of how its fits into that wider perspective - how its uniqueness becomes a factor in the total identity of Christian community and reflects the purposes of the whole from that particular perspective.

Qualify this complexity by the inevitable factors of imperfection and sinfulness, and the following picture emerges: particularity is part of what makes a community a community. When unique individuals are able to share their uniqueness and become united, the particular community thus formed is itself unique, and that uniqueness gives it an identity which reinforces the bond of unity. This unique particularity defines the community as different from other communities. Yet a particular Christian community will have particular vices, and these, like viruses, will not only self-replicate as the community maintains its identity from generation to generation, but will infect others along the way.[3]

SCRIPTURE AND COMMUNITY

A paper like this has to pull itself up by its bootstraps. So much has been assumed already about the relationship between Scripture and community in merely using the term 'Christian community'. How does a community justify itself as Christian without measuring itself by the yardstick of the Christian Scriptures? And yet to say that is to imply that we are able to assume an 'eye of God' view of both community and Scripture - as if we could as it were step out of our communal skins and relate to Scripture without the conditioning of communal tradition and likewise 'get at' a Scripture similarly unconditioned.

Yet this boot-strapping would happen at whatever point the discussion started. The complexity and 'fallenness' of human community and culture needs to be acknowledged whenever we affirm that Christian community is, by definition, community formed and redeemed in relation and obedience to Christ, and therefore framed by the Christian gospel.

Taking it, then, as a given that Christian communities share all the characteristics and shortcomings of human communities in general, and further that in some cases they are not communities at all in the true sense of the term, the project now becomes that of pulling all this into the encounter between community and Scripture.

If we revisit Lindbeck's assertion that this relationship is one of mutual interpretation, we might say that this interpretation begins with mutual questioning. Revelation emerges from a dynamic encounter between Scripture and tradition informed by reason. Implicitly I have been letting Scripture pose the question: what is Christian community? Scripture's own answers to that question are familiar to us all in the images or models of the Church we find in the New Testament, such as the Church as the body of Christ, with all its implications for understanding Christian community as Eucharistically constituted, and (not unproblematically) in the Old Testament understanding of the people of God subject to divinely-given rules for community living. To place both Testaments thus side by side immediately begs the question of what rules of interpretation we should use - not only in evaluating these models and rules, but also in relating Old and New Testaments.

The moment we get into this sort of discussion, however, we have turned the tables and the interpreting is going in the other direction. There is in fact no way that we can separate the two processes. The interpretation of a community according to Scripture is simultaneously the interpretation of Scripture according to that community. At the same time that Scripture questions the nature of community, the community asks the question at the heart of all reading and interpretation: what is Scripture for *us*?

To tease out this question I propose to go by a roundabout route. There is the labelling of a text as Scripture by a community and there is the use of a text as Scripture. There is what we call 'Scripture' and there is what we take to be Scripture for us. To call a text 'Scripture' is to refer to it as a sacred piece of writing. It is also to regard it as authoritative. However the two are not necessarily one and the same. In a paper entitled 'Reading a text as though it were Scripture', Wesley Kort observes that while 'it is the function of the role of scriptural texts to give persons and groups both a world and a sense of how to carry on in it', it is also true that 'the texts of beliefs and assumptions that enable and constrain the worlds of persons and groups constitute their Scriptures'.[4] The Scriptures we live by are not necessarily the ones we claim to be our Scriptures.

Thus the question what does it mean for a community to read a text as Scripture begs another. *Which* text does the community take as Scripture? Which biblical text according to which interpretation, or rather, as is always the case, which particular reading-into (of a community's own world of culture, belief and prejudice) into which reading-out-of the text? All is indelibly belief- and-culture- ridden.

To read any text as if it were Scripture means assenting to its truth, but not simply as factual truth. Scriptural truth is a complex thing, for our knowledge of it is more than conceptual. It is as much a matter of knowing how as knowing that - knowing how to go on, how to live our lives. As Kort points out, it is the capacity of Scripture to give us a world that makes it Scripture for us. Scripture is something we live within, according to the framework it sets for our reality, which means that we can work back the other way; we can discern what parts or aspects of the Bible, or what hybrid mix of biblical and/or other texts ('texts' actual or implicit) a community takes to be Scripture by observing its patterns of living. What we can be sure about is that every community, religious or not, has its Scriptures that it lives by.[5]

When we put all this alongside the earlier discussion of the complex particularity of Christian community, is it any wonder that while most of us may agree about the authority of Scripture - that Scripture has authority over our lives - we have difficulty in agreeing how we are to live by that authority. For each Christian community reads a slightly different text as Scripture.

How then can we understand one another?

It is important to hold on to the notion of mutual interpretation between Scripture and community and what that entails, which is openness. Gerhard Sauter has posed the question, 'what is the difference between standing upon the Bible and standing under it'? He notes that:

> People who emphasize standing upon the Bible wish to assert their steadfastness and religious accountability. Perhaps they want to affirm that they stand on solid ground, on the eternal Word of God, and not on the shifting views and changing opinions of human beings. But those who speak like this should see to it that they do not place themselves above the Bible and trample on it in the process. The Bible can never be beneath us. ... To place oneself under the

Bible means, on the contrary, to expose oneself to Scripture, to pay attention to what it has to communicate.[6]

To read the Bible as Scripture means to let it interpret us, the readers. This requires us to 'sit under' it in humility and openness, to let it expose our other 'scriptures' as idols, unconditionally accepting that it reveals and witnesses to a reality which, while we may do battle, question and struggle with it, is a reality beyond our limited and sinful minds and therefore must have the last word. Such acceptance is therefore not passive but actively engaging. It allows that our understanding is incomplete, that this reality we open ourselves up to is yet to reach its fulfilment in connection to our world and our lives. Yet, while this truth is above and beyond us it is nevertheless reliable, so we must trust it in our uncertainty and let it anchor our world-view and open up God's reality for us little by little. For it is the place where we dialogue with God, the locus of our relationship with him, in which we are placed in the context of his relationship with his people through the ages.

For Scripture to interpret the community is for the community to submit to the text. This is not in the sense of applying it as a rule-book, but in the sense of allowing God to do a new thing through this interpretation - to open up new facets of understanding pertinent to that community's situation. We repent of earlier idolatries. Again and again we attempt to grasp the fullness of the Word.

Redeeming the reading of Scripture

While the mutual interpretation of Scripture and community is limited and distorted due to human ignorance and sin,[7] the local community nevertheless has the potential to enable God's word to be rendered uniquely, if partially, through its perspective, or sum of perspectives. Each local interpretation is indispensably part of the whole kaleidoscope of interpretations. Each unique reading is the product of a community's engagement, over generations, with the divine gift to it of certain understandings and uses of Scripture. And as such it participates in God's presence in his world through his Word as witnessed in Scripture, some aspects of which are only able to be revealed and enacted by *this* people *here*.

Therefore, a particular community is called to read and practise the gospel in a new way, producing new insights and allowing the Spirit to do a new thing. In this way, Scripture has authority over the life of the community, as opposed to the community's use of the authority of Scripture to justify itself. As Sauter observes:

> We do not search to find what we already know, what we have been informed about for all time through a biblical instruction, but rather to come upon Christ in the pages and to hear him alone (*solus christus*) among all the voices; we encounter him anew time after time. "You search the Scriptures because you think that in them you have eternal life; but it is they that testify on my behalf" (John 5:39).[8]

What does it mean for a community to take Scripture as thus interpretative and renewing of its life and progressively shaping and reshaping of its world-view? Lindbeck and Tanner suggest that in the first place it is to take its meaning to be the 'plain sense', which is what makes sense in the context of communal reading, to the extent that this literal common-sense reading is found to be 'consistent with the kind of text it is taken to be by the community for which it is important'.[9] Yet in reading Scripture in terms of the 'plain sense', the community is also to read it 'through' Christ. To read Scripture for its plain sense, without falling either into fundamentalist literalism or selective convenience, requires us to return to the classical way of interpreting Scripture which reads all through, and in terms of Christ who is its unity, according to a Trinitarian rule of faith.[10] Thus 'what is Scripture for *us*', with all its dangers of bias and partiality, is redeemed in being read 'through Christ'.

Scripture and the redeeming of community

Yet, we may well ask: how can this redeeming reading of the plain sense of Scripture through Christ take place, when our Christian communities, more often than not, are locked into an endless unredeemed cycle of mutually reinforcing, self-replicating rules and practices - not to mention the idolatry of taking our partialness to be completeness? How is communal self-transcendence possible?

In John's Gospel, Jesus enjoins his disciples to love one another and promises them the help of an Advocate - the Spirit of Truth (John 11:26). Paul likewise talks of the Spirit coming to the aid of human weakness (Romans 8:1) and urges the communities he has founded to 'preserve the unity of the Spirit in the bond of peace' (Ephesians 4:3), to remember that by one Spirit they 'were baptised into one body' (1 Corinthians 12:13) and so to do everything necessary to build up that body. The community which is Christ's body with Christ as its head must work together, expressing a complementarity of gifts (1 Corinthians 12; Ephesians 4:1-16).

Within such a community, teachers and prophets may operate as redeeming agents in Christ, as the office of the (Old Testament) prophet is drawn within the framework of Christian community.

It is central to Christian belief that no true unity can exist apart from the Holy Spirit, who is the agent of Christ's reconciling work within human community. Christian communities are urged to let the Spirit work among and within them. Yet, on standing back from the content of the message, we find the person of the messenger, the one led and empowered by the Spirit to bring the message of reconciliation, the Apostle himself, involved in Christ's redeeming of communities. Communities that he himself founded are now suffering corruption from within and without. So he urges, teaches and visits them; he witnesses and testifies to the way Christians must lead their lives as persons redeemed in Christ.

CASE STUDY 3

During the regrouping and amalgamation of the parishes which now form Kilmoremoy Union (consisting of five parishes in north Mayo and south Sligo, in the diocese of Killala), the loss of local autonomy (in the form of separate select vestries with control of fabric and finances) was taken by parishioners to mean the loss of control and identity, and so greeted with fear and despondency.

However, as old select vestry memberships and traditions were changed with the formation of the encompassing union select vestry, this provided the opportunity for a new rector to set up new structures. These structures took the form of local parish vestry subcommittees, membership of which (while including elected select vestry members for that parish) was open to all parishioners. The scriptural vision of various unique members forming one body with complementary gifts and mutual accountability, bearing with one another in love, trust, and patience, was upheld as primary for both the select vestry and its local subcommittees.

The remit of the subcommittees, being wider than that of the select vestry, as well as more local, enables everyone to have a voice in regard to any aspect of church life. Being informal and consensual, the style is thus less threatening for those not used to having a voice. The rector reserves the right to chair to preserve neutrality and a wider vision. So far the result has been a unified new select vestry working in harmony; while at local sub-committee level, signs of democratisation, encouragement of those on the edge, the beginnings of a re-establishment of the positive aspects of past identity and vision, as well as provision of a forum for voicing continuing anxieties.

Here Scripture provides us with both message and model. We learn from this that central to the redemption of a community is the gift of sitting under Scripture with another; the gift of seeing ourselves and our community through the eyes of the outsider, the messenger sent by God. Sometimes the opportunity to receive this gift comes through changed circumstances, in which the community is taken outside of itself, in being removed from what is familiar and safe, and so becomes outsider to itself. If it can be enabled to resist the temptation to take ostrich action or lock itself into perennial lamenting for a lost Golden Age, such a crisis may help the messenger from outside to stand with the community outside of itself, to challenge its received view of Scripture and foster self-re-evaluation of the community's tradition(s) of interpretation.

The process of redeeming community requires openness and willingness to be vulnerable, to risk dialogue - perhaps at the expense of some things regarded as constitutive of Christian identity in this particular place - in order to discover just how we may truly embody Christ. Skilled facilitation is needed to help communities to 'use the difficulty' of threat to identity, and to find and share the positive aspects of the new identity rather than simply focus on the negatives of 'the other'. Then there are the risks of fore-closing (rushing to answers and applications before there has been adequate sitting under Scripture - especially where a community's identity has been formed in terms of a particular theological template for reading). Also some community members may preclude a dialogical reading by dominating the conversation or by simply failing to listen - talking past each other and so failing to touch 'worlds' at all.

Barriers to redemption

In all this we have to reckon with the following barriers to redemption:

● *Our world is the only world*
This barrier arises not only in situations of isolation and homogeneity in which community members have not travelled and their contact with outsiders has been limited. It is not only an expression of ignorance and insularity, but also an indication of a particular fallacy of modern thinking: the 'one size fits all' interpretation that does not take account of communal uniqueness or historical continuity, and mistakes the partial for the whole. My uncle, who for some years worked as an engineer in Papua-New Guinea, tells this story:

Christ being the 'cornerstone' of the Church conveys much to most Westerners but is meaningless to those tribes living in total isolation in the floodplains of the Western Province of Papua-New Guinea (PNG) [a vast area north of the Fly River where stone/rock is quite unknown]. While in PNG, we had occasion to host a Dr Price [who was] visiting PNG to assist translators working throughout the country through the Bible Society, and he used this dilemma to illustrate both the problem and his recommendation to those translating the New Testament into the languages of the several tribes native to this area. In this region houses are built with timber and reed grasses, and a ridge pole plays a vital role in keeping up the roof. So the name given by the locals to this pole has been used by the Bible translators rather than attempting to produce a name which would convey little. At a subsequent meeting of missionaries and church folk held in Port Moresby where this was elaborated upon by Dr Price, there followed much heated debate on his right to adulterate Scripture in this way![11]

Yet it must be remembered that partial-ness is also expressed in the inevitable loose-ends and discontinuities that disrupt the set patterns and certainties of a given community such as its understandings and uses of Scripture. Progressive re-ordering of those understandings and uses is required if the community is to avoid making an idol of its traditions and remain true to its Christian calling.

● *Patriarchy*

A faithful remnant of the 'old' community rules the community and is resistant to both change and the contribution of newer members. The dynamics are all too familiar and are often seen in parishes which have seen long and/or frequent vacancies. Because there is no genuine openness, this situation effectively blocks the input that is the first stage in redemption: the community's seeing itself as others see it.

CASE STUDY 4

Due to dwindling numbers and lack of leadership in a small New Zealand town parish community, one family increasingly assumed responsibility for the leadership of the community. This was done with the best of intentions: 'to prevent the doors closing' by people of faith who were prepared to put their commitment into action, and pay the cost of shouldering the burden of administration. Yet, the corollary of taking on such responsibility by a few was the apathy and lack of responsibility of the others, who were then able to 'enjoy' the destructive double luxury of not contributing and resenting those who did.

As the faithful few thus assumed more and more responsibility they became used to the power that went with the responsibility, and came to take it for granted. And so, unconsciously, a benevolent dictatorship was born. The 'church parents' ceased to consult and advise the others who seemed happy enough to leave it all to them. When newcomers came they were welcomed, but they were expected to know their place and fit in, and so were given no space to flourish. In the end the newcomers left. When I inquired about this parish recently, I was told the church had been closed.

- *Excluded middle*

This barrier refers to the sort of all-too-frequent oppositions and factions within and between communities in which only one, or neither, side is prepared to look for middle or common ground. This may be characterised by labelling, stereotyping, and accusing, with accompanying readings of the others' lives as negative parables, or cautionary tales. Tribal exclusiveness and polarising over issues may also lead to fear of contamination ('we won't have anything to do with people who believe or will tolerate *that*!') and to the fear of capitulation and takeover if one iota is conceded. In this situation a certain code of belief is taken as constitutive of identity and buttressed by appeal to Scripture. This may be the 'scripture' of implicit local communal rules (see pp 106-08), or the more explicit 'scripture' of a particular churchmanship, or, on its own or as extra weight to any of these, appealing to the biblical Scriptures themselves. In this latter case, such an appeal is an instance of the 'standing upon Scripture' referred to by Gerhard Sauter (see p. 117 above) who sees this as a besetting sin of 'Protestantism':

> [E]very 'justification' which is produced with the help of the 'principle of scripture' understands itself as something completely different; namely as *legitimation and authorization*. It is put forward as the ultimate, valid justification with a claim to

infallibility, as an unalterable point of departure and an unshakable foundation. In other words, it is presented as the *final substantiation* of everything Protestantism ever stood for. In this process both justification and scripture are fundamentally misunderstood, as if the Bible serves to *derive* religious values from divine revelation. These are, of course, assumed to be the values of Protestantism which is therefore, for this reason, to be accepted at the purest expression of Christian religion.[12]

● *Loss of 'apostolicity'*

The final and, I believe, most serious barrier to the redemption of community is the lack or failure of leadership, and in particular, the loss of 'apostolicity'.

The New Testament model of the apostle, as found in Paul and inferred from his letters, is very much that of the founder and redeemer in Christ of Christian community. As an itinerant trail-blazer, visitor, teacher, critic, and encourager, Paul acted as mediator between the worlds of different communities, cross-fertilizing, locating common ground, being 'all things to all people'. The apostle shows us the Christ who, as the creator and redeemer of human community, is the one who is the go-between, with one foot in the mire and one foot on the bank, the mediator between heaven and earth who, as such, can hold together alien, even opposed worlds.

Thus apostolic authority is itself granted by Scripture

while the apostle in turn enables the community to sit under Scripture. Apostolic authority is inextricably linked to the authority of Scripture; it can claim no validity if shorn from its origins in and responsibility to Scripture. As such, the apostle comes to our communities in the person of the outsider who steps inside, in the leader and teacher from elsewhere who comes to partake of and renew their life: to preach good news to their poor, to proclaim release for their prisoners, and recovery of sight for their blind (Luke 4:18-19; Isaiah 61:1-2) and then establishes and maintains local leadership to carry on the vision.

The limits of local interpretation and the role of the leader

Parish clergy and other local leaders may prove good facilitators, and newly-appointed incumbents or priests-in-charge may initially assume an apostolic ministry. In situations where the twin evils of 'patriarchy' and alienation have split a community, the arrival of a new leader may facilitate the redemptive agency of the 'blow-ins' while uncovering and reaffirming the original scriptural vision of the 'faithful remnant' which may have become so sedimented over with the accretion of home-grown tradition that the gospel is no longer visible.[13]

Yet all too soon, familiarity sets in and the apostle becomes instead local preacher, teacher and pastor. Apostolicity is essentially itinerant and trail-blazing, transcendent and visionary. Primary and essential to the process of redeeming Christian community, the apostle provides, facilitates and supports the kind of mediating leadership appropriate to the 'sitting under' of Scripture. This leadership challenges and enables local leaders to be prophetic voices of communal self-criticism. Then in turn the leader may enable individual members to critique the received view or offer prophetic insights and teaching (while in turn being answerable to the community and maintaining of its continuity and stability). These may be individuals who have experienced life in other communities, aware of alternative ways of reading and living the gospel, while choosing to make their home in this particular community. In this way, under apostolic guidance and visitation, the local leader may continue to operate as visionary, opening up a wider interpretation and use of Scripture, bridging factions and giving voice to the marginalised.

However, another reason why a rector or other local stipendiary minister cannot single-handedly perform the apostolic role relates to the limits of mutual interpretation between Scripture and community in one local setting. As mentioned earlier, the partial and particular world of the local community not only needs to be redeemed, but also complemented by the perspectives of other communities. For the mutual interpretation of Scripture and community to allow the Spirit to do a new thing, a 'stereoscopic vision' is needed. As David Kamitsuka, quoting Lindbeck, remarks:

> so long as the "basic rules" for scriptural use remain the same, differing plain senses can be viewed... "as the fusion of the self-identical story with the new worlds within which it is told and retold".[14]

In other words, differing interpretations across communities may be seen as alternative parables illustrating the same text, providing a complex, three-dimensional view of that text when these 'parables' are shared through reading the Bible together inter-communally, sharing interpretations and insights, discussing interpretations, communicating consensus and disagreement, and finding common ground of agreement (however small) from which to explore difference.

Application

The practical 'how' of the mutual interpretation of Scripture and community may be seen to be demonstrated by people spontaneously voting with their feet and forming small cross-community groups which gather to 'sit under' Scripture. In admitting no divisions and sharing faith in a fundamental way, these may resemble the 'base communities' of Latin America.

CASE STUDY 5

The Greek class meets weekly on a Wednesday afternoon at Canon Mark's house. The group (which regularly comprises two Roman Catholics, two 'Church of Ireland-ers', and two Methodists, while others come and go) is reading through Matthew's gospel. Today the discussion has strayed on, as it is inclined to, to the lectionary readings for the following Sunday. Canon Mark likes the way 'living water' connects word and sacrament. We go back to Matthew chapter 5. The word for 'altar' is derived from the word for sacrifice.

'I notice your Church doesn't emphasize the sacrifice of the mass,' remarks Canon Mark to me, after we have discussed altars and communion tables. When I agree, he quotes from the words of institution at the last supper. 'Yes, that seems to confirm that Jesus himself was talking about sacrifice,' I say.

Across the room, one of the Methodists in our group nods his head. We leave the doctrinal issues hanging for the time being.... We pray about what we have shared together before we leave.

Groups like the Greek class (as outlined above in case study 5) succeed best when they are not issues-based. Sitting under Scripture across community boundaries resembles the conversations that take place while walking, gardening or washing up: the Spirit is able to work while our anxieties are momentarily stilled. In this way each community may be the agent of the others' redemption as differing perspectives are worked through in the light of Scripture. Exploring the 'why' of differences leads to greater mutual and self-understanding which in turn opens up new insights in reading together. The result is mutual respect even where there are irreducible areas of disagreement. The witness of true Christian community - or at least the beginnings of it - occurs through such a sitting under Scripture.

Yet wherever such groups exist, they do so because there is a 'Canon Mark' (as in case study 5) with a vision for such interaction. What of situations where such visionary leadership is not forthcoming?

In this day and age, we are inclined to reach for corporate private-sector methods and set about inventing new job descriptions, new posts, and training of various kinds for leaders. Under such an influence the thought occurs to me: why not train and commission a group of roving facilitators who would not only initiate such cross-community interactions, but also establish and support the leaders maintaining these groups? If their work were local and personal enough, invoked by incumbents and bishops as the necessity arose, this would avoid the sort of 'top-down glossy programme syndrome' that is inclined to provoke something akin to 'donor fatigue' in rectors and parishes.

Yet it is not as simple as that. The dilemma is that these roving persons, however well trained, commissioned and recommended, would need to have local standing and authority as well as neutrality and ability. Then the thought occurs also that apostolic leadership is an *episcopal* job-description. While we cannot rule it out that the Spirit may give apostolic gifts to others, generally to talk of apostolic leadership is to talk of bishops, who of course have the signal advantage of standing with one foot in our respective camps, while still being a neutral influence from outside the local community - with recognised authority to preach, teach, admonish and encourage. Instead of having too many bishops (as is often said, usually with financial considerations in mind) does the Church, in fact, have too few who are therefore too bogged down with administration and meetings? Does not a scattered, and in some places, divided Church need *more* episcopal oversight rather than less, in the form of assistant bishops in each diocese - whose primary ministry is to exercise the sort of apostolic leadership that operated in the early Church?

Summary and conclusion

This essay began with George Lindbeck's notion of the mutual interpretation of Scripture and community, which I then complicated with an extended discussion of the nature of community in general and of Christian community in particular. I identified the need for Christian communities to be open to Christ's work of redemption. I suggested that such openness needed to begin with the repentance that comes from a self-critical awareness of the 'natural' implicit 'law' of the community as a hidden factor of unity, which in various ways, and reinforced by the influence of the wider culture, may undermine and obstruct that redemption, promoting exclusion of others and creating scape-goats upon which to foist its collective sin. For this reason the opportunity and ability of some of us to be itinerant Christians, or at least to step outside our natal communities and see them from the perspective of another location, whether geographical or conceptual, is a vital aspect of the redemption of community.

I noted how the uniqueness and diversity of human community, as God-given aspects of the goodness of creation, are vital factors in the total identity of Christian community as it seeks the Kingdom of God. Due to this uniqueness and diversity, each community reads and practises a slightly different text as Scripture. Therefore such seeking must involve the sitting under Scripture humbly and together, being open to each other's reading and offering mutual encouragement, critique, and respect. In such 'sitting under', the common text provides the continuo that is capable of holding together very different, even opposing 'parables' of interpretation.

The application of such sitting together requires not only a physical meeting across communities, whether within or between traditions, but also the sort of visionary and facilitating leadership that will be able to deal with communal barriers to redemption and openness and thus bring together diverse and opposing interpretations in a way that gives the Spirit space to open up new insights in relation to both Scripture and community. I have suggested that such leadership is essentially apostolic in nature and as such has its origins in and accountability to Scripture. This carries the implication that, in the light of the urgency of working on helping opposed factions in the Church of Ireland to talk and listen to each other, a review of present Church structures might be indicated. Finally, I have also suggested that such meeting will work better if it is not issues-based, but simply involves a coming together in small inter-communal (or in some cases intra-communal) groups to read the Scriptures together, with the preparedness to go where the Spirit leads in discussion, worship, and prayer. Community is, in the final instance, communion - Eucharistic, and as such, ultimately to be fulfilled when Christ is all in all.

References:

1. George Lindbeck, 'Scripture, consensus and community', in Richard Neuhaus (ed.), *Biblical interpretation in crisis* (Grand Rapids: Eerdmans, 1989), pp 78-101.
2. See Bruce D. Marshall, 'Absorbing the world: Christianity and the universe of truths', in Bruce D. Marshall (ed.), *Theology and dialogue* (Indianapolis: Notre Dame, 1990) pp 69-95.
3. See Marjorie Hewitt Suchocki, *The fall to violence: original sin in relational theology* (New York: Continuum, 1999), pp 120-1.
4. Wesley Kort, 'Reading a text as though it were Scripture', draft paper presented at the Center of Theological Inquiry, Princeton, March 1994. See published work: Wesley A. Kort, *'Take read': scripture, textuality and cultural practice* (Pennsylvania: Penn State University Press, 1996).
5. *ibid.*, pp 5-6.
6. Gerhard Sauter, 'Scriptural faithfulness is not a "scripture

principle'", in Gerhard Sauter and John Barton (eds.), *Revelation and story: narrative theology and the centrality of the story* (Burlington VT: Ashgate, 2000) pp 7-28, at p. 7.
7. Kathryn Tanner, 'Theology and the plain sense', in Garrett Green (ed.), S*criptural authority and narrative interpretation* (Philadelphia: Fortress, 1987), pp 59-81.
8. Sauter, *op. cit*, 'Scriptural faithfulness is not a "scripture principle"', p. 7.
9. David Kamitsuka, *Theology and contemporary culture: liberation, post-liberal and revisionary perspectives* (Cambridge University Press, 1999) pp 120, 123. See also Tanner, *op. cit.*, 'Theology and the plain sense' p. 62.
10. Lindbeck, *op. cit.*, 'Scripture, consensus, and community', p. 77.
11. Personal communication, October 2004.
12. Sauter, *op. cit.*, 'Scriptural faithfulness is not a "scripture principle"', p. 7.
13. See Tanner, *op. cit.*, 'Theology and the plain sense'.
14. Kamitsuka, *op. cit.*, Theology and contemporary culture, p. 8.

For further reading:

Laurie Green, *Let's do theology* (London: Continuum, 1990)
Stanley Hauerwas, *Vision and virtue* (Indiana: University of Notre Dame Press, 1981)
Garrett Green (ed.), S*criptural authority and narrative interpretation* (Philadelphia: Fortress, 1987)
Richard Neuhaus (ed.), *Biblical interpretation in crisis* (Grand Rapids: Eerdmans, 1989)

5

THE ETHICAL 'USE' OF SCRIPTURE

Nigel Biggar

THE VERY FIRST thing to say about our use of Scripture is that our use of Scripture is not the first thing. Before we use Scripture, Scripture forms us. We only pay attention to it at all because we have first been convinced that it tells some very important truths about the nature of things. We only regard it as an authority supreme among human authorities because we have been convinced that the truths it tells are basic ones, truths upon which our views and our lives ought to be founded.

Formation before use

Among these are the basic truths that the evolving universe is maintained and guided by an intelligent, benevolent, effective, and super-human Creator. That the created universe is designed to culminate in the emergence of creatures who are capable of responding consciously, voluntarily, and with joy to the beauty of this good and rational 'God'. That the emergence in human creatures of a peculiarly high level of consciousness gives rise to a tension between the appetites proper to their nature as animals on the one hand, and the aspirations and callings proper to their nature as *human* animals on the other. That it also produces a constant and dreadful awareness of death, as well as a capacity to imagine alternative futures and therewith the burden of responsibility for discerning the best option from the better and the worse. That the pain of bearing the tension between animality and humanity, the dread of death, and the fear of the burden of moral responsibility all create the occasions for sinful attempts at flight either from the creaturely constraints of our animality into a ruthless asceticism, or from the responsibilities of our humanity into a childish obliviousness. And that God so cares that we should fulfil our destiny that he has taken action to save us from futile, self-violating flight by wooing us with compassion through Jesus, by showing us in Jesus the beauty of a life where human aspirations govern (without repressing) animal appetites, and by giving us hope through Jesus' resurrection that death need not reduce us and all that we have built to dust.

These truths, to which Scripture bears witness, are basic to a Christian view of things; and part of this is the Christian vision of what a good human life looks like. Long before Scripture furnishes us with resources to use in thinking through, for example, moral questions about homosexual practice or moral quandaries about the taking of human life, it locates us in a certain reading of things that forms the basis of our moral vision.

First, to believe in a 'Creator' of the world is to see the latter as intended to realize desirable goals or 'goods'. Accordingly, the 'created' world implies a world designed to produce (human) beings capable of appreciating, caring about, maintaining, and promoting things-that-are-good-in-themselves - such as truth, beauty, and moral virtue. 'Creation', then, is structured by a seeking after certain values. It is characterized by a moral order that precedes, and provides the context for, human choosing. By so placing us in a created world, the biblical narrative refuses to radical moral relativism and moral nihilism the status of rational options. Moreover, it asserts that the first word in ethics is 'good', not 'law'. 'Man is not made for the Sabbath, but the Sabbath for Man': human beings do not exist to serve the law; rather the law exists to serve the human good.

Second, to believe that 'sinfulness' characterizes the condition of human beings is not, according to Scripture, primarily to hold them guilty of immoral acts. 'Sin' is not primarily about extramarital sex or the use of the 'f-word'. In the first place it is about our estrangement from our God-given calling to live in appreciation and service of what is intrinsically good and worthwhile in the created world. What has caused this estrangement? A combination of fear and its offspring, sloth. The dread of death demoralizes us, impelling us to flee the burden of responsibility that our human calling to serve the goods of creation places upon us, and to attempt to bury ourselves in animal obliviousness with the aid of alcohol, sex, drugs - and shopping. By so placing us in the condition of sin, the Bible renders us skeptical of the modern diagnosis of human ills that lays them all at the feet of poverty and ignorance; and of the complacent liberal assumption that ever-expanding freedom from social constraints is bound to march hand in hand with a growing care for human dignity. We know that the root of human ills lies more deeply in the existential anxiety of mortal creatures, and that human salvation requires an awful lot more than the extension of individual choice.

Third, to believe that the Creator of the world reacts to our self-violating attempts to flee human responsibility with the sad eye of compassion rather than the wagging finger of reprimand, is to take the wind out of the sails of our bristling self-justification and to open us out to the possibility of salvific change. And to believe that the Creator has raised from the dead one who, trusting in God's fidelity, remained utterly faithful to his calling to serve the goods of creation in spite of the injustices heaped upon him, is to blow the wind of hope into the deflated sails of our moral resolve - for what has graced one virtuous man could well grace others like him. By so placing us in relationship to the compassion of God, and to God's resurrection of Jesus from the dead, the biblical story remoralises us. It frees us to let down our defences and acknowledge that we're in a mess, caught between a high human calling that intimidates us and a merely animal obliviousness that cannot satisfy us. It also energizes us, giving us reason to hope that, if we answer our human calling to spend our lives in the service of the goods of creation - and thus in worship of the Creator - death will not bring us, and all that we have invested in, and all whom we have learned to love, and all that we have built, to naught.

The very first thing that Scripture tells us about our use of Scripture, then, is that before we use it, it has already formed us. It has shaped our basic understanding of the world, of the situation of human beings, and of the moral life. Given the biblical narrative, we take it for granted that moral life is about believing that the resurrection of Jesus was an event that happened to Jesus before it happened in the psyches of his disciples. Thus it is about trusting in the benevolence and power of God, about hoping that death will not be the last word spoken to all our moral efforts, and about committing ourselves to the service of the goods of creation - maintaining them, defending them, and promoting them. In this way, before we even think about using Scripture to figure out what we should and should not do, it has already endowed us with beliefs that give us the elements of moral deliberation (e.g. objective goods or values), and attitudes of faith and hope that generate and sustain moral energy.

The need for responsible construction

When we do turn to Scripture for help in figuring out what we should think about, say, homosexual practice or non-therapeutic cloning, or whether we should or should not support the war against Iraq or the remission of 'Third World' debt, it is important to remind ourselves what Scripture is not. Scripture is not a manual of ethics. It does not furnish us with a coherent ethical system that can be applied to ethical problems to produce the right answer. Rather, Scripture is a compendium of theological texts, written over a millennium by dozens of different authors in dozens of different situations. Of course, these texts contain ethical principles and rules, and morally exemplary stories; and sometimes what one text says about moral matters is the same or similar to what others say. But not always. Sometimes a biblical text presents the indiscriminate slaughter of a people - genocide - as commanded by God (I Samuel 15). Then another text enjoins the reader to withhold himself not only from vengeance, but from any violent retaliation against enemies at all (Romans 12:19-21). And then yet another assures the reader that the 'sword' has been ordained by God for use by public authorities in the suppression of wrongdoing (Romans 13:4). At one moment a biblical author (St Paul) tells us that in Christ the social distinction between man and woman - as between Hebrew and Greek, freeman and slave - has been abolished (Galatians 3:28); but at another, the same author enjoins wives to be subordinate to their husbands (Ephesians 5:22-24). The surface of the text of Scripture does not furnish us with a ready-made, coherent system of ethics. If we are going to have a coherent system - and we surely need one if our moral judgements are not to be whimsical - then we will have to build one out of the text. We will have to construct one.

To say that we must 'construct' an ethic out of Scripture implies that Scripture must become material in our intellectual hands - it must become subject to our thinking, to our logic, to our judgement. That this should be so, however, is not unbiblical. In the opening chapters of its very first book, the Bible presents human beings as graced with the special dignity of being made in the 'image of God' (Genesis 1:26). Among the various things that this has been held to mean, one of the most exegetically sound reads it in terms of the 'dominion' that human creatures are given (in the very same verse) to exercise over the rest of creation. To be made in the 'image of God' is to be given the responsibility - and the powers - of a vicegerent: human beings are to manage and develop creation on God's behalf. This implies that humans are not just puppets or robots or minions. If God makes them in his 'image' and gives them 'dominion', then they have room for (relatively) independent manoeuvre. They have the freedom, within responsibility, to make their own diagnoses and to invent their own remedies. They have the freedom, within responsibility, to think or to reason. And since Scripture does not present them with a ready-made ethic, they must exercise that freedom, within responsibility, in constructing a coherent ethic out of the biblical text.

There is no evading the point that such construction does involve the subordination of Scripture to 'reason'.

But it need not amount to Scripture's subordination to an *alien* 'reason'. Certainly, we have to think - to reason - about how to build an ethical system out of Scripture. And this will inevitably involve having to decide to give more weight to some parts of Scripture than to others. It might also involve having to contradict some parts in the name of others. But such decisions and judgements need not be made on the basis of considerations *foreign* to Scripture itself. To take an obvious and uncontroversial example, there are surely good theological reasons, easily grounded in Scripture itself, for giving the New Testament a certain priority in the construction of a Christian ethic. Accordingly, to say that the need to construct an ethic out of Scripture involves the subordination of Scripture to 'reason' is to put the matter too simply and invite misunderstanding. The more complex truth is that it involves the subordination of Scripture to a 'reason' that has already been informed by Scripture itself. If there is 'subordination' here - and there is - then it is not subordination to an enemy.

We cannot avoid the interpretative construction of Scripture. This is one of the responsibilities to which we are called as human beings, and we ought to resist the temptation to take sinful flight from it into subhuman intellectual slavery. On the other hand, none of us really builds from scratch. All of us come to Scripture with a set of theological and ethical beliefs and convictions that we have inherited or acquired from particular tradition(s) of Christian thought and practice. We come to Scripture with a set of theological and ethical constructions that our forerunners in the faith have bequeathed us - constructions that owe something to Scripture itself, something to the concerns of their authors, and something to the theological and philosophical traditions in which they stand. And it is through these constructions - be they conservative evangelical, 'open' evangelical, Barthian, Anglo-Catholic, liberal, or Cupittian - that we are immediately inclined to make coherent sense of the pluriform text of Scripture. It could not be otherwise. We humans are not gods, but creatures - embedded in history, formed by historical traditions, moved by the concerns of the day.

Still, we are *human* creatures. We do have the power - and the responsibility - to think again about what we have received and owned. We do have some capacity - God-given - for detaching ourselves from, rising above, and looking critically down upon our cherished theological and ethical assumptions. We have some capacity, that is, for rational self-transcendence. What is more, if we are to approach Scripture in a manner consistent with what the biblical and subsequent Christian traditions say about human being and the human condition, then we must approach it with the humility of creatures who know that their understanding is limited and fallible, and with the humility of sinners who know that their understanding is distorted by selfish anxieties and interests. Because of our human responsibility, our creaturely limitations and fallibility, and our sinful corruption, then, when we approach Scripture we should do so in a manner that is open to hear things that may not easily fit our theological and ethical preconceptions; and that is ready, upon rational reflection, to suffer correction. We never meet Scripture as *cartes blanches*, and we need to be aware of that. We always meet it already equipped - or, as it may turn out, encumbered. It could not be otherwise for creatures bound by time and space. But that is not to say that we cannot meet Scripture openly, honestly, ready to listen, ready to hear what we do not expect, ready to learn something new. Is this to 'use' Scripture? In a sense, yes, it is; for we are using Scripture to test our current assumptions, our reasoning, and our conclusions. In the end, we may still stand where we stood at the beginning, but, thanks to the thinking that Scripture has provoked, knowing the place far better. On the other hand, our encounter may persuade us to shift our feet onto new territory.

Either way, Scripture does not merely tell us what to think. It provokes a process of reflection, in which we reason as well and responsibly as we can. In a certain sense, we do 'use' what Scripture says - we chew it over, we seek the best way to make sense of it. But that is not to say that we 'use' it just as we please.

Encountering Scripture: two illustrations

So far, so abstract. Let's endow the point with flesh and blood. Suppose that you are a conservative evangelical and you come to Scripture with the controversy about homosexual practice on your mind. Very likely, you come with some ready-made convictions: you are convinced that the Bible is the supreme and decisive authority in the Church, and you are convinced that homosexual practice is against the will of God.

To some extent your view of homosexual practice is based upon your conviction about the authority of Scripture. But there are other factors at work, too. Your reading of what it is that Scripture says has been shaped by the knowledge that post-biblical traditions - Catholic, Reformed, and Roman Catholic - are all unanimous in condemning sexual relations between persons of the same sex. It has also been shaped by the popular argument - recently developed by the New

Testament scholar, Robert Gagnon - that the occasional expressions of disapproval of homosexual practice that one finds in Scripture have a deeper rationale: namely, God's intention that human individuals should find fulfilment by engaging with a sexual 'other' in a relationship of complementarity.

And now you come to Scripture. What is it that you want? It would be quite natural if you were to want to find confirmation of what you already believe. But presumably, had you been absolutely certain of what Scripture says, you wouldn't have taken the trouble to return to it. So the fact that you're here facing Scripture again means that, even if you want reassurance that what you already believe is correct (who among us doesn't?), you are nevertheless willing to hear something at least a little different. You have come to hear the Word of God, and not merely the echo of your own voice.

So what might happen? Well, first of all it may occur to you that no human tradition - not even the Reformed tradition - is sacrosanct; and that one of the main lessons of Jesus' career is that it is precisely those who hold rigidly fast to religious and theological tradition who stand in danger of missing the presence of God and of blaspheming against God's Spirit. Next, as you reflect on what Scripture has to say about homosexual practice, you might notice that the number of occasions on which biblical authors say anything about it can be counted on less than two hands - and none of these occasions is more than a verse or two in length. Then you might notice that reasonable arguments have been made that on several of these occasions what is being commented on is not homosexual practice *as such* but homosexual rape or cultic prostitution or pederasty. So, on reflection, the immediate biblical basis for the moral disapproval of homosexual relations *as such* shrinks to a mere handful of verses, most notably Romans 1:24-27. Now arises the obvious question: can such a very narrow biblical base be made to bear so much moral weight? To this the reasonable thought may enter your mind that, yes, the narrow base can bear the weight, if the rare expressions of outright disapproval can be seen as occasional tips of a submerged iceberg of rationale. In other words, behind the rare condemnations of homosexual practice lies a deeper point of principle.

What might this be? One currently popular proposal is that St Paul's conception of what is 'natural' in Romans 1:24-27 should be understood in the light of Genesis 1:27 ('So God created man in his own image, in the image of God he created him; male and female he created them'). That is to say, human beings are made to grow and to flourish *in the encounter between the sexes* - male with female, female with male - and that homosexual relations are therefore 'unnatural' because they avoid the mutually enriching meeting with the sexual 'other'. This is the so-called 'complementarity' argument.[1] If this were indeed the deeper rationale for Scripture's rare explicit condemnations of homosexual practice, then it would certainly give the latter more weight and force. But suppose that, upon reflection, this does not make very good sense? In order to make its case against homosexual relations, the 'complementarity' argument has to claim that heterosexual relations are universally normative - that they constitute *every* human being's path to maturity. It also has to claim that non-sexual forms of encounter between the sexes do not suffice, since many practicing homosexuals enjoy intimate, platonic friendship with members of the opposite sex. But what does this imply about those who are destined to remain single through no fault of their own? Are they fated to remain stunted in their humanity? And what does it say about the early Christian ideal of virginity or about the Christian notion of a vocation to celibacy? Besides, in what sense are those who engage in heterosexual relations supposed to be more mature in humanity? Even if such relations do hold out special possibilities of human enrichment - and doubtless they do - why are they reckoned to be so essential to human flourishing that no other social relationship can provide an adequate substitute? After all, parties to a homosexual relationship encounter more than mere mirror-images of themselves. If satisfactory answers to these questions are not forthcoming, then it would seem that the complementarity thesis creates more problems than solutions. And if that is the case, can you - in all conscience - continue to hold to it?

Let's take another example. Suppose that you are a 'liberal' Christian and you come to Scripture with the Iraq war on your mind. You come with the visceral conviction, born of human experience, that all violence is an evil and that to take part in it is wicked.

You regard Scripture as a major authority in that you recognize the virtue of Jesus' ethic of compassion and non-retaliation, of an 'option' for the poor and marginal, and of prophetic criticism of oppressive 'powers', and you see in this ethic the power of the divine Spirit by which the world will be saved. You also believe that in the first three centuries after Jesus' life and death the Christian Church remained faithful to his moral example, but that when Constantine first tolerated and then established Christianity as the imperial religion in the fourth century AD, the Church sold out.

And now you come to Scripture. Certainly you come with your convictions and beliefs, but perhaps these are also attended by niggling doubts. It does seem to you, for example, that sometimes atrocious regimes cannot be dislodged except by resort to armed force. Perhaps you suspect that, were it not for military intervention in Kosovo and Iraq, Slobodan Milosevic and Saddam Hussein would still be in power, ruthlessly suppressing domestic opposition and recklessly exploiting nationalist fervour - and that they would continue to do so for years to come, unhindered by a divided and ineffectual international community.

Equipped with such certainties and propelled by such doubts, you come to Scripture. What might you find? On the one hand, lots of material comes rushing out to confirm you in your assumptions - Jesus' teaching about compassion and forgiveness, his vocal opposition to oppressive religious and state powers, his own refusal to retaliate and St Paul's injunction that all Christians should follow suit (Romans 12:17-21). On the other hand, perhaps with the help of St Augustine or St Thomas Aquinas, you notice in the Gospels (e.g. Matthew 8:5-13) and the Book of Acts (chapter 10) the occasions on which Jesus or his disciples have dealing with Roman centurions, and that on none of these occasions are the soldiers urged to give up their military profession.

Maybe too, prompted by Martin Luther, you begin to wonder how reasonable it is to assume that Jesus' teaching and example applies to the conduct of civil government - as distinct from private, interpersonal relationships. And then it occurs to you that the very fact that some of the early Fathers of the Christian Church took the trouble to argue that the military profession is incompatible with Christian confession, implies that not all of their Christian contemporaries agreed with them -indeed, Tertullian's famous treatise on the subject, *On the military wreath*, was provoked by an incident involving *Christian* members of the Roman army.[2] But if that is so, then just how pacifist was the pre-Constantinian church? And at this point you remember that while in the twelfth chapter of his Epistle to the Romans St Paul urges his Roman *confrères* to 'repay no one evil for evil' and to leave the taking of vengeance to 'the wrath of God' (12:17,19), a mere six verses later he insists that the governing authority or ruler 'does not bear the sword in vain; he is the servant of God to execute his wrath on the wrongdoer' (13:4). So just how much consensus was there among the original Christians that Jesus' teaching and example applies straightforwardly to the public as well as the private realms?

What is the general point of these two extended examples? The point is to show that when we come to Scripture in search of help in thinking through some ethical - or doctrinal - question, we do not 'use' it in the sense of finding there either a ready-made answer or a technical method of producing such an answer. We do not 'use' it in the way that we use a resource or a tool. Rather, we 'use' it in the sense that we allow it to provoke our thinking - our reason - into posing a series of questions to our current convictions and assumptions, including those about what we should take Scripture to *mean*. We 'use' it to test what we already think, perchance to modify or even correct it. Our 'use' of Scripture, then, involves above all an honesty about what we already think (and feel) about the matter that concerns us, together with an openness - only proper to sinful creatures - to hearing the Word of God tell us something we hadn't expected.

Hearing while thinking in the Church

This 'hearing' of God's Word does not occur in an empty space of purely passive listening. It occurs as we *think* about the biblical text and what it means. It occurs as we *reason*. It occurs as we *act* intellectually. This is only as it should be for creatures graced with the dignity of a commission to manage creation. On the other hand, the fact that we act upon the text of Scripture need not mean that the text itself is reduced to passive matter, mere putty in our rationalising hands. After all, it is possible to think in a manner that also listens. Indeed, if we reason responsibly, then we will reason humbly. As we reason, we will let Scripture speak, raising doubts, posing questions, suggesting fresh lines of thinking. Our reasoning will take the form of a responsible dialogue - one in which we take seriously both what we already think (for, given our rationality as *imagines dei*, we might be right) and what challenges us to think otherwise (for, given our fallibility as sinful creatures, we could be wrong).

But this dialogue is not a private one. It does not just involve my individual reasoning and the biblical text. It already involves 'tradition'. For what I already think has inevitably been shaped by some reaches of Christian tradition. If I am an evangelical, the chances are high that my convictions and beliefs will bear the heavy stamp of St Paul, St Augustine, Luther, Calvin, and some of the more recent expressions of conservative Reformed thought. If I am liberal the chances are that my thinking will be impressed by the ethics of the classic prophets in the Old Testament and of Jesus in the Gospels, by 'anti-establishment' streams of Christian tradition such as the Anabaptists and the Quakers, and by modern schools of thought such as liberation and feminist theology. And if I am Anglo-Catholic my views will typically be most shaped by the Early Fathers, by St Thomas Aquinas, by the 'just war' school, by Christian socialism, and by Catholic social teaching. So when we come to Scripture we bring Christian traditions with us, and as we reason with the biblical text the voices of our forerunners in the faith enter into the dialogue.

But if our reasoning with Scripture involves historic tradition(s), it also involves the contemporary Church. When we come to Scripture to test what we think, we come with fragments of sermons or segments of audio-tapes or passages of articles or books echoing in our minds. And maybe we do not come alone. Maybe we come to Scripture as part of a Bible-study or discussion group, and when we reason we do so aloud and in the company of others. Thinking need not be solitary. And when we think sociably, we dialogue with the living as well as the dead.

Some may find this account of our 'use' of Scripture

far too vague and elusive - far too impractical. After all, it does not furnish any tools by which we can unlock the truth. But that's because the truth isn't like that - or at least not the truth about how we should live our lives. It isn't an object waiting to be captured by the correct technique. By calling the truth 'the Word of God', we signal that we ought to approach it, not as miners approach a coal-face, but as pilgrims approach a shrine. If we would know the truth about how we should live, then we must seek it in accordance with the kinds of beings we are: not mini-gods, but finite, fallible, and sinful creatures; and yet not mindless puppets, but creatures dignified with a commission to reflect the Creator in using their heads to manage the world for its own good. We may not possess a certain method, but we have been given a suitable manner - responsible, honest, humble, and sociable. And if we adopt this manner as we reason about the text of Scripture, then we can be confident - since God is good - that in our reasoning we will hear yet more of his Word.

References:

1. For a classic version of this interpretation, see Karl Barth, 'The doctrine of creation' in *Church dogmatics, III,* part 4 (Edinburgh: T. & T. Clark, 1961), particularly at p. 166, more generally pp 163-68. For the more recent version developed

by Robert Gagnon, see his *The Bible and homosexual practice: texts and hermeneutics* (Nashville: Abingdon, 2001); and for a debate about this version, see Robert Gagnon and Dan Via, *Homosexuality and the Bible: two views* (Minneapolis: Fortress, 2003). I owe thanks to Dr David Atkinson, the Bishop of Thetford and Dr Kevin Ward of the School of Theology and Religious Studies at the University of Leeds for alerting me to the current popularity of the complementarity thesis among those who oppose the normalisation of homosexual relations.

2. After the death of the Roman emperor Septimius Severus on 4 February 211, his two sons followed the custom of bestowing on each soldier in the army a gift of money. Military regulations required the recipients of this gift to wear a crown of laurel on their heads. One soldier refused to do this because, as a Christian, he did not consider himself permitted to take part in a heathen rite. The soldier was arrested, thrown into prison, and condemned to death. His case provoked Tertullian (*c.* 160-225AD) to write against Christian participation in military service.

For further reading:

John Barton, *What is the Bible?* (London: SPCK, 1997). See especially chapter 6, entitled: 'Biblical morality', pp 92-109

Bruce C. Birch and Larry L. Rasmussen, *Bible and ethics in the Christian life* (Minneapolis: Augsburg, 1989)

Richard B. Hays, *The moral vision of the New Testament* (Edinburgh: T. & T. Clark, 1996)

Allen Verhey, 'Bible in Christian ethics', in James F. Childress and John MacQuarrie (eds.), A *new dictionary of Christian ethics* (London: SCM Press, 1986), pp 57-61

idem., *The great reversal: ethics and the New Testament* (Grand Rapids: Eerdmans, 1984)

SIX THESES ON SCRIPTURAL AUTHORITY

1. HOLY SCRIPTURE IS THE inspired and definitive witness to the revelation of God in Christ. For Christians it is the supreme authority in all matters of faith, order and conduct. This normative authority was and is not *conferred*, but rather was and is *recognised* by the Church.

2. THE CHURCH'S DIALOGUE WITH Scripture is to be understood in terms of the demands that it places upon us who 'sit under it', and not in the sense that it is under our control.

3. HOLY SCRIPTURE IS PROPERLY understood by the Church when the person and work of Christ is held as the interpretative key, and its authority is mediated to us via Christ and the apostles.

4. HOLY SCRIPTURE IS UNIFIED in its message, and the Church is called through the Holy Spirit to re-appropriate this message in every age.

5. WITH REGARD TO HOLY SCRIPTURE, we fully affirm the sixth of the Thirty-Nine Articles of

Religion that:

Holy Scripture contains all things necessary to salvation: so that whatsoever is not read therein, nor may be proved thereby, is not to be required of anyone, that it should be believed as an article of the Faith, or be thought requisite or necessary to salvation.

6. THE AUTHORITY OF HOLY SCRIPTURE is neither diminished nor undermined by the full rigours of critical scholarship.

Postlude

As was suggested at the outset, the purpose of this document is to point to a place where reasonable and courteous dialogue on the nature and authority of the Holy Scriptures may become a reality.

Whether this has been accomplished will be established only by the results which may be achieved. It is our hope that these essays and the theses which emerge from them may be discussed widely within the Church of Ireland, whether in parish groups, clerical societies or in adult education seminars.

The Holy Scriptures were given to humankind for the most constructive of all purposes - as a route map towards salvation in Jesus Christ. For this road ever to have become a battleground is surely a device of evil. We pray that our report may give some modest nourishment for those who wish to travel the road in love and charity with their fellow pilgrims.

✠ **Richard Meath and Kildare**